IT'S MUCK YOU...

IT'S MUCK YOU WANT!

The humorous story of a double life

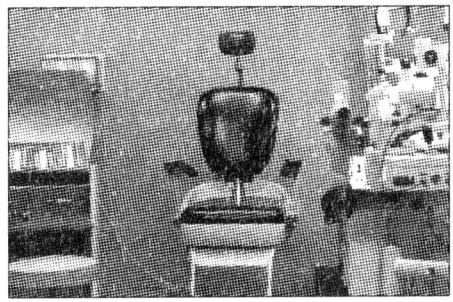

JACK ORRELL

To my darling wife Sheila
Who persuaded me that 'anyone can write a book'
J.O.

ISBN
1 901253 41 4
First published June 2004

© Jack Orrell 2004

The moral right of Jack Orrell to be identified as the author of this work has been asserted by him in accordance with the Copyright, Designs and Patents Act 1988.

All rights reserved. No part of this publication may be reproduced, stored in a retrieval system, or transmitted in any form or by any means, electronic, mechanical, photocopying, recording or otherwise, without the prior permission of the copyright owner.

British Library Cataloguing in Publication Data.
A catalogue record for this book
is available from the British Library

Published by:
Léonie Press
an imprint of
Anne Loader Publications
13 Vale Road, Hartford,
Northwich, Cheshire CW8 1PL Gt Britain
Tel: 01606 75660   Fax: 01606 77609
e-mail: anne@leoniepress.com
Website: www.anneloaderpublications.co.uk
www.leoniepress.com

Printed by:
Anne Loader Publications
Collated and bound by: B & S Swindells Ltd, Knutsford
Covers laminated by: The Finishing Touch, St Helens

Jack Orrell, aged 88

ABOUT THE AUTHOR

Jack (the name he has been known by since childhood, although he was christened 'John Edward') was born in Walton, Liverpool on June 2nd, 1915. His father, who was a Sergeant in the R.G.A., was killed on the Somme in 1917, so Jack was raised in a household consisting of his mother, her spinster sister, two half sisters, an African green parrot, a Sealyham and two Pekinese dogs. Sometimes the cacophony of confused sound got him down, so he developed a protective 'Deaf Ear' which he sometimes malpractices on his wife, Sheila – much to her annoyance.

He went to Alsops High School in Liverpool and enjoyed a happy but uneventful childhood. Life changed suddenly when his elder sister Eileen married. Her husband, Ron, a 6ft 'He-man', became his hero figure. He taught Jack so much – a knowledge of the countryside, fishing, shooting and a love of motor bikes and then cars.

He trained him in the art of self-defence, and even tried to convince Jack's widowed mother that he had a future as as prize fighter. An uncle thought Jack should follow his example and be a dentist. This was abhorrent to Jack who wished to be a motor mechanic. Eventually a compromise was reached and he became an optician.

The most important thing Ron taught him was that whatever task you set yourself, it should be done to perfection. This is a practice to which he has adhered all his life.

CONTENTS

Chapter 1 – Childhood memories	1
Chapter 2 – My queer relations	10
Chapter 3 – Summer holidays	14
Chapter 4 – The love of motorcycling	17
Chapter 5 – Deciding on a career	23
Chapter 6 – Early years	28
Chapter 7 – Time to move on	33
Chapter 8 – War clouds gather	37
Chapter 9 – Start of a new life (Brook House)	44
Chapter 10 – Riding adventures	48
Chapter 11 – Massey House Farm – we take a gamble	62
Chapter 12 – The move to Massey House Farm	67
Chapter 13 – Motors	86
Chapter 14 – Rats	91
Chapter 15 – The yard	98
Chapter 16 – Veterinary work	100
Chapter 17 – The caravan	105
Chapter 18 – On the way up	108
Chapter 19 – Free spectacles	111
Chapter 20 – Experimental poultry unit	113
Chapter 21 – A delayed journey	124
Chapter 22 – The mad cow	126
Chapter 23 – The village fete	127
Chapter 24 – Working days	132
Chapter 25 – Night out	135
Chapter 26 – Search for a new hobby	138
Chapter 27 – A change of heart	151
Postscript	162
Appendix i – Transcript of sale catalogue 1951	180
Appendix ii – Transcript of auction proceeds 1961	184
Appendix iii – Plan of Massey House Farm buildings	188

LIST OF PHOTOGRAPHS

Jack Orrell pictured sailing, in his sixties	viii
Sheila - blue-eyed blonde	83
Jack on honeymoon in Wales	83
Portrait taken on embarkation leave	83
Staff Sgt Orrell in the Middle East	84
Baby Anne at Brook House	84
Sheila and Anne in garden of Brook House	84
Anne and Richard at the seaside	85
Sheila and Jane in the garden of Massey House Farm	85
Massey House farm (2 views)	86
George, Colin and Athur	87
Mrs Teggin	87
Arthur, collecting eggs	87
Bull pen and shippon	88
Part of shippon	88
Fred the Ayrshire bull	89
Fred's progeny	89
Experimental poultry unit (3 views)	90
Richard and Anne helping their father	91
On holiday at Llangranog	91
J. E. Orrell Ophthalmic Optician (3 views)	92
Ford Zodiac, 3.4 Jaguar, Allard, Mark VII Jaguar	93
MGB GT, Granada 3ltr coupé, 280SL Mercedes, E-type Jaguar	94
'Tamba', 'Golden Eagle', 'Water Music' and 'Magic Dragon'	95
'Magic Dragon', 'Coquette', 'Jansfin'	96
'Fiddler of Orwell, Sheila the crew, skipper Jack aged 70	97
'Caldy Wood' (2 views)	98
Garden at 'Minnows'	98
Jack celebrates his 85th birthday in June 2000	178

Jack Orrell pictured sailing, in his sixties

CHAPTER 1

CHILDHOOD MEMORIES

I first opened my eyes on June 2nd, 1915 – not an ideal time to enter this world. Great Britain was in the throes of a fight to the death with Germany and the cream of our manhood were being killed in their thousands. My father, who was aged about 23, had already joined the forces and was in France with his regiment. He was a sergeant in the Royal Garrison Artillery.

My mother was of Welsh parentage. Her parents had apparently run a large butcher's shop in the centre of Chester. Forsaking the family business, she became manageress of a tobacconist and sweet shop and in addition was a model for one of the popular artists of the day. I never was told the full story, but somehow she ended up with two small illegitimate daughters.

My uncle, her brother, was a dental surgeon in Walton, Liverpool and my mother, after training, became his assistant.

My father was a member of a prominent Liverpool family. His great grandfather, John Napoleon Orrell, had built himself quite a little empire. His main interest seemed to be building: he had a large building firm and his own brickworks. To this day there is an extensive area in Liverpool called Orrell Park which his firm built. He also was the owner of a brewery and various wine and spirit outlets. On the lighter side, he apparently had interests in the Rotunda Theatre in Liverpool and the Argyle Theatre in

Birkenhead, and used to sit in his box, complete with top hat and stick, and if he didn't like one of the acts he would just wave them off.

John Napoleon spread his wealth between all his relatives, but unfortunately they mostly seemed to be interested in wine and 'wimmen.'

My father had a brother and a sister, and they all came in for a share in the booty. I never remember meeting his sister, my aunt, but it appears that she had a disastrous arranged marriage – so she eloped to the Isle of Man with her true love and disappeared into obscurity. Uncle John, his brother, bought a farm in Aintree, and my father spent a lot of his time there helping out. He was very fond of animals, and was trying to sort out what to do with his inheritance when war was declared.

One fatal day he had toothache, so he made an appointment to see the local dental surgeon, who turned out to be Herbert Roberts, my mother's brother. When he arrived at the surgery he was of course greeted by my mother, who advised him to go into the parlour and relax for a while after his treatment. Whilst he was relaxing, her two tiny beautiful daughters were allowed to stray in and entertain him.

My mother was auburn-haired and a strikingly beautiful woman. She certainly knew what she wanted, and it wasn't long before she had him on the way to the altar. He must have been about 21 and she was several years older. He adopted Eileen and Mixie, and left them an equal share to myself in his will.

As an investment for some of the money which he had inherited, my father bought a row of eight terraced houses in Haggerston Road, Liverpool and it was in the end one of these that I was born. The houses were substantial four-bedroom premises and at that time faced a wide open common, which was many years later made into an attractive public park.

The block of houses was rented out, and the family moved to a larger house in Queens Drive.

In 1916 my mother received the terrible news that her beloved husband had been killed in action and that she was left alone to rear and provide for three small children. She sold the Queens Drive house and moved once again, this time to 24 Walton Village. Once more this was a four-bedroom terrace house, but this time it had two large attics. It was situated immediately opposite the Rectory, an enormous great house with extensive gardens that was occupied by Archdeacon Spooner – a most impressive figure who, complete in black frock coat, gaiters and black bowler type hat, used to be seen on the odd occasion ministering to his flock.

Walton Village at that time really was a village, a number of houses still had thatched roofs and there were two small farms and a dairy just down the road.

The church was very much part of the community. It had a full peal of bells and chimed the hours – it also had an ancient set of punishment stocks.

Next to the church there was a small church school which was only 100 yards from our house. This was a rather depressing place as there was no greenery surrounding it, just a stark concrete playground enclosed by 8ft high iron railings. There was a large meshed metal gate at the entrance and a most doleful metal bell which sounded like the one on the old Newgate Prison. When it was time for school, this used to start ringing, and gradually go faster and faster for the last minute, at which time the metal gate was slammed to and a large chain and padlock secured around it. Woe betide any child who arrived late, for they were locked out and had no option but to slink home in ignominy.

When I was five years old it was decided that it was time I started school and so arrangements were made to send me to this institution. I was absolutely terrified: every time the bell started ringing I used to lock myself in the lavatory and have to be literally dragged out.

Corporal punishment was very much the thing in those days, and even the five-year-olds used to have their knuckles severely rapped for the slightest misdemeanour.

After a fortnight of misery, my mother suddenly found that my hair was full of head lice. The school was free, so naturally some of the poorest children in the village had been sitting next to me and had passed on some of their livestock. That was the end of my stay at the Church free school.

It was then decided that I should be sent to the kindergarten of the school which my two sisters were attending. This was a small college called Miss Clarke's, in the grounds of a large house. There were masses of rhododendron and hydrangea bushes, and large green lawns where the children could play.

I was put in the charge of Miss Eileen, who was a pretty, gentle sort of person, and I soon began to enjoy going to school.

As I got a little older I acquired a scooter, in fact all the boys in the class had scooters, and we regularly ran furious races home when the dismissal bell sounded.

When I had been at the school for three years one of my school mates contracted Scarlet Fever, from which he died. To my mother's great concern I started to show signs that I had got the dreaded disease. At that time there were no such things as antibiotics and Scarlet Fever was a real killer.

Strict precautions had to be put in place immediately. I was confined to the best bedroom, a blanket soaked in disinfectant was hung over the door, and nobody except my mother was allowed in the room. Every time she went out of the room she had to change her dress and wash in a bowl of disinfectant. A lovely coal fire, burning day and night, was my only comfort. I was seriously ill for months, but gradually began to recover.

When the doctor considered that I was no longer infectious, the health authorities had to be informed so that they could decontaminate the house.

The long black fever van arrived with its crew dressed in black waterproof suits. All the curtains and blankets were removed and burned, all my precious books and toys were confiscated, and the bedroom was filled with disinfectant smoke bombs and sealed for a day.

When I was fully recovered, it was decided that it was time that I went to a boys-only school, so I was enrolled at Merton School for Boys – a small establishment run by Mr and Mrs Tollett, who were both Oxford graduates.

This school was again run in a large old house with a big garden, of which Mr Tollett made full use. He grew all his own vegetables and also had a large poultry unit, where in play breaks he could be seen collecting eggs and occasionally slitting the throat of a cockerel which he had decided to have for his dinner.

Mr Tollett was quite an impressive figure. He was about 6ft 3ins tall with a bald head, and wore a pair of 'pince nez' spectacles on the end of his nose. Apparently he was a former Oxford Blue. His classroom, which overlooked the garden, was a very well-organised affair. He had constructed a platform about 3ft high on which his large flat-top desk rested, this platform reached right back to the wall on which there was a full-scale map of the world and two blackboards. To the left of the blackboards three different-sized canes were hung up. From this elevated and dominant position he rigidly controlled the destiny of his small pupils. Fortunately, he was a mild-tempered man, and made his lessons so interesting that I can never remember him having to reach out for the canes at his rear.

Mrs Tollett used to take over his class for an afternoon a week and instruct us in various practical pursuits, including wood-carving, basket-weaving and picture-framing. Another afternoon each week we used to ride our bicycles down to Seaforth sands and play hockey – this was organised by our athletic headmaster who acted as referee.

After the match and on our way home, we would call in at a special sweet shop for bottles of pop, and sweets at 4oz for a penny. In the summer we were taught the rudiments of cricket.

There was no television to distract and drive us indoors, and our outdoor play was simple and wholesome.

There was a great wide pavement by the churchyard wall, which was in the next street to our house, and this used to be one of our play areas.

'Whip and top' was the favourite game of the day. Tops came in a great many shapes and sizes. Firstly, there were the turnip tops: these had a flat top, about 3ins in diameter, and then straight sides leading down to a steel point on the bottom. The tops of these had patterns drawn on them, using pieces of coloured chalk. A thin leather thong was wrapped around their side, and with a quick movement of the hand they were set spinning.

My two sisters, Eileen and Mixie, were enthusiastic top-spinners and on most nights it was quite a sight to see a crowd of youngsters spinning their multicoloured tops.

The other popular top was a very different shape: it had a rounded top and a long straight side. This was a real firework, and if given a fierce stroke with the whip would rise 6ft in the air and land in a crazy spin.

Wooden and metal hoops, and skipping ropes, were also very popular and provided great exercise.

I enjoyed my years at Merton School for Boys, but when I reached the age of 11, it was once again time to move on.

The best school in the district was Alsop High School, entrance to which was governed by an examination. This I somehow managed to pass, and in the autumn I took up my position there.

Alsop's was a very different type of school. It had about 500 pupils and every master had an MA or MSc degree. Mr Halford, the headmaster, was a highly-qualified intellectual and always remained a somewhat aloof and unapproachable figure. He ran the school with the utmost efficiency and was undoubtedly proud of its achievements. He had a French wife, so was very keen on French. He took us for French lessons on a Saturday morning when we finally reached the sixth form, otherwise the only other time we came into contact with him was at the end of the term when punishment was being handed out.

The school ran an American system of stars and stripes. If you managed to acquire 10 stripes – which could be handed out for bad work or misbehaviour – you automatically at the end of term reported to the headmaster, who delivered six of the best. Stars were awarded in quarters and one quarter would cancel out one stripe. A full star could merit a half day's holiday at the end of term.

It has always struck me as being an excellent system, and was readily accepted by the boys. We certainly never had any instances of teachers being attacked, as is now prevalent in the present era of do-gooders.

The school had excellent chemistry laboratories, a tuck shop, gymnasium and a very good public swimming baths only 200 yards away.

Each year a Gilbert and Sullivan opera was performed for the public, and included our own full orchestra.

I enjoyed my school days to the full, had lots of friends and certainly made the most of my spare time.

Liverpool at that time was a live and vibrant city: it had a wonderful system of electric tramcars which encompassed the whole of the city and its outskirts. The tramcars were double-deckers; each had a driver and a conductor who collected the fares. For two pence you could go for miles. One of my frequent excursions was down to the Pier Head where the famous Liver Building stood with its great clock and the great Liver birds perched on top. It used to fascinate me to walk along the waterfront.

All the streets in Liverpool were cobbled. The tramcars travelled on a double steel track in the centre of the road, and other traffic ran on either side of them.

The road back from the Pier Head to Walton was through an impoverished district called Scotland Road. The road ran parallel to the dock area, where thousands of tons of molasses and animal food were stored, so there was a constant pungent odour in the background.

The district was the home of a very large Irish contingent, who worked mostly on unloading and loading cargoes on the docks. There was a pub on nearly every street corner, and as a result poverty was indigent.

The womenfolk were known as 'Mary Ellens' and wrapped themselves in grey shawls, somewhere in which resided a small infant.

As the tramcars rumbled and squealed their way up the road, large wagons with steel-rimmed wheels, loaded with produce and drawn by teams of fine horses, crashed and banged alongside on the cobbles.

It was a pitiful, lawless sort of area and Saturday night, when the men drew their wages, was riot time. Beer flowed like water, and of course it all ended up with the usual fights. Poor half-starved, bare-footed children and their mothers could be seen waiting outside the pubs to try and get their menfolk home before they were knocked unconscious or had spent the last penny of their wages.

My Raleigh All Steel Bicycle was my most treasured possession and in those far-off days gave endless enjoyment. Most Saturday nights my pals and I used to cycle about a couple of miles to one of the cinemas which took our fancy. These were the days of the silent cinema so if possible we would try and find a film which had special effects. These were usually carried out by the pianist who used to sit underneath the screen and with whips, sheets of steel, guns and buckets of water, he would try to emulate what was happening on the screen. It was frequently very amusing when he got the sequence wrong.

When we came out, it was great fun, in the dark, trying to get our acetylene lamps to work. Simple oil lamps were the easiest but they only gave out a very feeble light. The acetylene lamp had a top chamber which was filled with water, the flow of which was controlled by a drip feed on to the dry acetylene powder beneath.

The tricky bit was to gauge just the right amount of water to provide the gas to the burner. If it was just right it would produce a brilliant white light, but if you overdid it you could blow the whole thing up.

By the time I was 11 years old, I decided that I wanted a racing bike. My mother was dead against it, as she thought that the low handlebars would make me round-shouldered. Nothing daunted, I thought the best thing was to try and make one. I went around all the local scrap yards and eventually acquired a rusty frame for five shillings. Over a period of time I gradually acquired all the bits and pieces necessary, so I sand-papered the rusty frame and painted it a brilliant yellow. The wheels were painted bright red, and the rest of the components assembled. I could only afford a front brake, but as it had a fixed wheel gearing it didn't seem to matter. It had no mudguards, of course, but it did have very low handlebars.

My mother was appalled, but my pals were green with envy.

CHAPTER 2

MY QUEER RELATIONS

When I was wandering around on my bike I used to call in occasionally to see my father's aunt, Mary Birch. My father's mother (my grandmother), had two sisters – Mary Birch who was the widow of a corn merchant and Mrs Reynolds who was the widow of the Chief Veterinary Surgeon to Liverpool Corporation.

The three sisters were all very different characters, and were all confirmed widows, dressed in black.

Mrs Birch lived the life of a recluse in a big old semi-detached house in Orrell Park, shutting herself up in the house and sometimes refusing to see anyone. At one time she used to keep hens but very often she would forget to feed them and the poor things would be found lying dead all over the garden. I was sorry for the old girl and used to call in and cut the grass with a rusty old mower. She never gave me any pocket money but would allow me to pick a few apples off her trees.

It was a fascinating house. She had never thrown anything away and the upstairs rooms were packed to the ceilings with pink newspapers from World War I and musical instruments of every description. I was warned by my mother never to eat any food if it was offered, as I would probably be poisoned.

Mrs Reynolds was a very different character. My mother took

me to see her on several occasions – hoping, I think, that as her dead nephew's son she might leave me something in her will.

She lived in the country out at Knotty Ash, in a large detached house surrounded by steel railings. By the side of the house there was a stable block with a carriage house and grooms' quarters.

When we rang the bell the door was opened by a maid dressed in apron and headdress. We were put in the lounge to await the arrival of the illustrious lady. A quick look around showed that the room was full of priceless antiques.

After a few moments my great aunt appeared and greeted us. A dainty tea was served by the maid.

Mrs Reynolds was convinced that she only had a short time to live and so she had ordered a special silk-lined coffin. She showed us the clothes in which she wished to be buried and also the hymns she wanted to be sung at her funeral.

To our amazement, she also showed us that she had put labels on every article in the house, directing to whom they were to be bequeathed.

On her demise, I imagine one of my unscrupulous relatives must have removed the labels, as I never did receive the pair of beautiful bronze horses which I was assured had my name on the label underneath.

My paternal grandmother was another crazy character. My grandfather had been a wine and spirit merchant in quite a big way and they had lived in a luxurious mansion next to Everton football stadium. Apparently they were in the habit of giving gigantic parties with champagne flowing like water – and then my grandfather died, and my grandmother went 'broke'.

When I was taken to see her by my mother, she was living on her own in a tiny farm cottage. There appeared to be only one room and this was dominated by a big table which was draped in a large green velvet tablecloth. Underneath the tablecloth a large snarling sheepdog was chained. At the far end of the room there was a monkey which ran backwards and forwards, chattering away and occasionally hurling pieces of apple at us.

The only other furniture in the room, apart from a few chairs, was an old upright piano.

When we were about to leave, my grandmother opened the lid of the piano and to my surprise produced a single bar of Cadburys Milk Tray chocolate, which she solemnly handed to me.

I don't remember ever seeing her again.

Unfortunately both my maternal grandparents had died before I was old enough to remember them.

Mary Birch did come up trumps in that she financed a tour of the French battlefields for the three of us as she wished to see her nephew's grave.

We went down to Dover by train, and then across to Calais. The tour took us to Amiens, Arras and the Menin Gate, and included a general walk around the underground trenches. It must have been depressing for my poor Mother to see the terrible conditions under which our soldiers had had to exist.

My father's grave was in Balliol Communal Cemetery, south west of Bethune, and we had to engage a taxi in order to find it.

As far as the eye could see there were hundreds and hundreds of little white gravestones. The whole of the area was immaculately kept, and it was a most impressive and moving moment for us.

My mother had come prepared with a lovely big sheaf of spring flowers, which she tenderly lowered onto the grave of her dear man who was only 24 when he was killed.

Mrs Reynolds, due to her late veterinary connections, used to receive grandstand tickets for the magnificent horse shows which were held outside St George's Hall. She didn't want to go herself, so she would send us the tickets.

This was the age of the horse and there were only very few motor vehicles about.

The Show started at 10am, and lasted all day. It was mostly a heavy horse show and Clydesdales, Suffolk Punches, Percherons and other breeds all vied with each other for the major prizes.

There were hundreds of magnificent animals on show and each and every one was groomed to perfection. Their manes and tails were plaited with gleaming straw, entwined with rows of flowers.

Not only were the horses beautifully decorated, there were also farm carts and enormous dray wagons each representing a different theme, such as the Ovaltine wagon which had a gigantic brown egg, a Friesian calf and a bevy of pretty dairymaids on board. All the popular brewers were represented by brightly-painted wagons covered with beer barrels and drawn by a team of lovely big Clydesdales.

Afternoon tea used to be served on the Terrace, and my mother and I really enjoyed the day.

CHAPTER 3

SUMMER HOLIDAYS

When school broke up for the summer holidays the whole family prepared for the annual visit to Rhyl. The party consisted of my mother, her spinster sister Lily, who was permanently living with us, my two sisters, who were now attractive teenagers, and myself.

My mother rented the same suite of rooms each year for four weeks. The rooms were in a boarding house situated on the promenade, and the landlady was a Mrs Vaughan.

Mr Vaughan and his two sons had two 'charabancs' which were parked opposite the house and they would spend their days trying to entice the passers-by to go on one of their mystery tours.

The 'charabancs' had solid rubber tyres and were open affairs. You certainly had a wonderful view and got plenty of fresh air. It was fine provided it didn't rain but at the first sign of a shower it was necessary to stop and erect the enormous hood, a complicated process which took about 15 minutes.

Each morning my mother and Lily would sally forth to the shops and come back laden with the day's victuals, which were handed to Mrs Vaughan who turned them into our daily meals.

Rhyl in those days was an ideal place for a family holiday. It had a safe sandy beach with a daily sandcastle competition for the children, an open air pierrot show, two theatres, and an excellent amusement park with a large lake, which a miniature railway used to circle every half hour. Another delight was to be rowed across the estuary by the Voryd boatman and witness the superb displays of trick riding given by the Cossack Horsemen.

Eileen and Mixie, my two sisters, of course were not interested in any of these things. They had just discovered that there were such things as boys.

The first thing they would do on arriving was to dress up in their latest finery and walk up and down the promenade hoping to make a 'catch' – which, being strikingly pretty girls, they soon did.

My mother used to lock them in their bedroom at 9.30pm, but unbeknown to her, it wasn't long before they had opened the bedroom window and jumped down into the arms of their boyfriends.

Eileen, the eldest, and my mother's favourite, fell madly in love with a character named Ron Smith, a bank clerk in the National Westminster Bank. Dressed in an ex-dispatch rider's tatty leather coat, breeches and boots, large leather gauntlets and a check cap, he used to charge up and down the promenade on his flash motorbike which had a 'straight through' exhaust.

Eileen was besotted by him. When we went home my mother told her that at 18 she was much too young to be tied down, and forbade her to see him. It was obviously the wrong approach as a few months later she ran away from home and married him.

It was some time before Ron was welcomed into the fold, but it did come to pass and after several short appointments at different branches of the bank they eventually ended up in West Kirby, where they rented a nice flat overlooking Dee Lane.

West Kirby is an attractive seaside resort nine miles from Birkenhead and it was a natural sequence that as a 13-year-old I would get on my racing bicycle, take the ferry to Birkenhead, and cycle out to visit them.

I was welcomed with open arms and was soon spending most of my spare time in West Kirby.

Ron Smith was a natural with children. He was a big tough-looking bloke with close-cropped hair – a man's man – and quickly became my hero. I suppose in a way he took over the role of the father I could not remember.

He taught me how to make a powerful and inexpensive catapult out of branches cut out of the hedgerows. He taught me how to catch a fish just using a bent pin and a bit of cotton. He taught me how to shoot.

Ron had been an enthusiastic boxer in his youth. He spent many hours with the gloves on teaching me the art of self-defence and when he thought that I was good enough, matched me against the local junior champion. In the third round I all but knocked him out. Ron was elated and tried to persuade my mother that I ought to take up a career in boxing.

She was not amused and quickly squashed that idea.

CHAPTER 4

THE LOVE OF MOTORCYCLING

Ron's pride and joy was his motorbike, which was a 490 ohv Norton. Everything on it had to be absolutely perfect and every little item which could be polished absolutely gleamed.

He kept this bike in a little shed in Price's Yard which was close to their flat. It was a meeting place for all the village lads who really cared about motorbikes.

Motorbikes in those early days were much simpler and more fun than they are now. Amateur tuning mostly consisted of polishing the ports and pistons, fitting stronger valve springs and experimenting with higher compression ratings.

Today's superbikes have taken all the joy out of amateur tinkering and are best left alone unless you possess all the necessary special equipment.

I was dying to get myself a motorbike and one day news came on the grapevine that in someone's back shed there was an old machine which might be going cheaply. When we located it, it turned out to be a two-speed belt-drive Campion and the price was 30 shillings.

I paid the money and the bike was towed back to Price's Yard for inspection. It was in a pretty rough state, so we decided to strip the whole thing down and do a major overhaul. I learned a lot about engines by the time we eventually got it reassembled.

I was only 13 and a motorbike licence in those days was issued at age 14, so I had a year to wait before I could get it on the road. I started my motorcycling hobby by taking it on the piece of waste ground opposite Price's Yard, occasionally pushing it down Dee Lane and onto the beach and riding it over to Hilbre Island. The only snag was that the sea water made the belt slip, and I had to keep stopping to put sand on the pulley. It was always a challenge knowing when it was safe to come back, as the police used to hide in the bushes in the hope of catching me.

The Campion was not very reliable and kept refusing to start, so Ron persuaded me to do a level swop with one of the gang for a single-gear belt-drive Levis. This was a sure-fire starter, but being single-geared with no clutch you had to run with it to start – and make sure that the throttle was not too far advanced or it would take off and leave you sitting on your bottom in the middle of the road.

The week before my 14th birthday I part-exchanged my Raleigh All Steel Bicycle for a 490 ohv AJS which cost £4 10s 0d.

I waited with impatience for the Road Tax to drop through the letter box and five minutes afterwards was tearing up Grange Hill flat out.

By the time I had acquired my motorbike, my mother had decided to move to West Kirby.

We moved to a brand new four-bedroom house in Salisbury Avenue, which was a completely new road leading down to the promenade.

I was of course delighted with the move, the only snag was that I had still got two more years to go before I completed my education.

Getting backwards and forwards to school was no easy task. Firstly, I had to take a steam train from West Kirby to Birkenhead Park, then I had to transfer to an electric train which ran under the Mersey to James Street Station, Liverpool. Once in Liverpool I had to board one of the electric tramcars which passed through Walton on its way to Aintree.

It was vital to catch all the connections and I rarely completed the journey in under two hours. It wasn't too bad in the summer but horrible on a bitterly cold morning in the winter when it was pouring with rain.

In those days, we used to have to go to school on a Saturday morning, so one Saturday I decided to go on my motorbike. Unfortunately I had a slight accident and arrived at school with one leg ripped out of my trousers.

To get to Liverpool with a bike it was necessary to cross the River Mersey, which entailed boarding one of the small steamers which carried cars, lorries and cattle. The approach to the ferry was down a steep slippery slope. It had been raining, and I must have hit an oily patch – anyway, my big powerful AJS suddenly shot from under me and I landed on the cobbles with a badly grazed knee and the right leg out of my trousers.

There was no real harm done to the bike, apart from a badly twisted footrest.

When I arrived at school Matron was very concerned and bandaged up my knee. She even stitched up my trouser leg.

Ron, my brother-in-law, was dead keen on all sorts of sport, so we used to take frequent trips to New Brighton to watch boxing and all-in wrestling matches.

When I approached my 16th birthday, which was the legal age for obtaining a car licence, I began to explain to my mother how desirable and useful it would be if we had a small car. I soon won her over and we acquired our first car, an Austin Swallow saloon. It was shaped a bit like an egg and was painted in two shades of light blue. It was two years old and I think had probably had quite a hard life.

Seventy years ago there were no driving tests so I just got in it and drove. What wonderful days – with traffic-clear roads, no speed cameras and petrol a shilling a gallon…

Having had my motorbike on the road for a couple of years, I soon became a proficient car driver and it wasn't long before I decided that it would be a good idea to take my mother for a trip to London. We booked in to stay at the Bedford Hotel in Southampton Row.

I managed to get to London and we arrived in Piccadilly Circus. I had no idea where Southampton Row was, so I parked the car by the Regent Palace and strolled over to the doorman to get directions. Just imagine trying to do that today!

We had an enjoyable week in London, saw a couple of shows, and 'did' all the places of interest. My mother began to think that the car was a good idea.

Flushed with the success of our London expedition, I decided that a tour of Devon and Cornwall should be our next aim.

We broke the journey by spending the first night in Tewkesbury, where we stayed at the famous Bell Hotel. The next night was spent at Dulverton at The Swan. We thoroughly enjoyed going around all the small coves, and finally ended up in Lynmouth. That is where disaster struck.

I put the little Austin into bottom gear and, with the footbrake hard on, managed to negotiate the long steep Countisbury Hill which leads down into Lynmouth. After we had had a nice lunch and a good look at the shops, it was time to leave.

The exit to the other side was up Lynton Hill. I didn't know it at the time, but Lynton Hill is a well-known and dangerous trial hill. Anyway there it was, looming up in front of me.

I could see by this time that it was very steep and had a vicious left-hand bend right at the top. I let in the clutch, revved the engine to its maximum through all the gears, and made a charge. I was just about managing it until I reached the bend, by which time I was in bottom gear and gradually going slower and slower. The next thing was that there was an ominous smell as the clutch gradually started to slip. The smell gradually got stronger and stronger, and soon there were clouds of smoke as the clutch burned out.

With no forward drive, we gradually started to roll backwards. I pressed as hard as I could on the footbrake and pulled the little handbrake up with both hands, to no avail – we were still sliding backwards. I tugged on the handbrake with renewed vigour. All of a sudden there was a bang and the thin cable which connected it to the tiny rear brake drums snapped in half. The footbrake only operated on the front wheels, so we rapidly started to increase our backwards momentum.

By this time my mother had begun to realise that we were in grave danger and started to scream her head off.

I had to make an instant decision – try and steer backwards down the hill, with the risk of overturning (there were no seatbelts in those days), or make an immediate turn before we went any faster, and crash the back of the car into the wall. I decided on the latter option.

The spare wheel was mounted on the back of the car, so it did to a certain extent cushion the impact and no serious damage was done.

I calmed my mother down, took her for a cup of tea and arranged with the local garage to collect the car, reline the clutch and fit a new brake cable.

We spent the night in Lynmouth and they had the car ready next day.

I didn't know at the time that there was an alternative and easier way out. Having learned my lesson about the limitations of an Austin Swallow, I took it!

Our adventures on this trip hadn't ended yet, though.

On the long haul back from Devon, we finally reached the Wirral at about 9pm. It was beginning to go dark, so I switched on the headlights.

The immediate effect was that the ignition cut out and the engine stopped.

I don't think that I had had the car out in the dark before, so I was totally unaware of this phenomenon.

Fortunately we were near to Two Mills Garage so I drove in and asked them if they could do anything about it. They were just about to close for the night, so we had no option but to leave the car there for the night and get a taxi home to West Kirby.

My mother was not amused.

Afterwards, I spent many happy hours tuning and improving the little Austin Swallow – hours which ought to have been spent studying for my school-leaving certificate...

CHAPTER 5

DECIDING ON A CAREER

I would dearly have liked to have been a motorbike mechanic but my mother wouldn't entertain the idea. Her brother was a dental surgeon and both my cousins were at university studying to become dental surgeons, so she wanted me to become one, too. I was appalled at the idea of spending the rest of my life inflicting pain on people, so I scanned around desperately trying to think of a profession which would placate my mother and which I should be happy with.

One day my mother decided to have her eyes examined for some new glasses, so she made an appointment to consult Mr H. Scholes, who had an optical practice in rooms over a large confectionery shop in The Crescent, West Kirby. When she got home she said what a good examination she had received and what a nice man Mr Scholes was.

It suddenly struck me that this might be a profession worth considering.

I asked her if she could find out from Mr Scholes what all the requirements were to gain the Fellowship of the British Optical Association.

I was told that first of all I should require a School-Leaving Certificate with passes in at least five subjects, which must include physics and mathematics.

Unfortunately, at school we had had a maths master who had 'lost his marbles'. The tale was that his wife had left him and that he was full of grief. Personally I think he had got the beginnings of Alzheimer's Disease, as some days he would sit at his desk and not speak a word for the entire lesson. Before leaving he would write on the blackboard a number of sums for our homework. Not having been instructed how to do them, we were obviously in trouble and soon lost interest.

As a result of this lack of teaching my knowledge of maths was abysmal and I had to have special tuition on the subject.

My mentor was a Mr Bertie Robinson. Bertie was really quite a character. He was about 50 years of age, and lived with his mother in a big ramshackle old house in Rock Ferry.

Rock Ferry is what is known as a 'has been' area. In days gone by the Riverside Mansions were owned by ships' captains and slave traders. It's said that the cellars in some of the houses still have ring bolts in the walls, to which the slaves were chained at night.

Bertie had an Oxford MSc degree but was one of those people who had opted out of the rat race. He was a brilliant photographer and cartoonist. He used to trundle around the area on his old bicycle and unearth things like the remains of old railway lines, which he would photograph, tracing their pathway underneath churches and their reappearance the other side of a chemist's shop.

He had the ability to make maths really interesting and I soon lost my dread of the subject.

The table in the front dining room, which he used as his study, was usually piled high with reference books and the only source of heat on a perishing December morning was a small gas stove, ceremoniously lit on my arrival by his 93-year-old mother, who still taught small children the rudiments of the piano.

Bertie and his mother were both cat lovers, and the combination of gas fumes and cat pee could at times be somewhat overpowering.

I can remember on one morning I had finished my lesson and was about to leave, when Mrs Robinson came in and sat down at the piano with her current small pupil. When the child struck the first few notes, there was a terrific screech and a large ginger tom suddenly shot out of the open top of the instrument.

It really was a madhouse, but they were both harmless and enjoyed their way of life.

To get back to my optics, it appeared that at that time I had two options.

I could either take a full-time two-year course at Manchester University, followed by a year with a qualified optician, or I could be apprenticed to a qualified optician for three years, during which time I should have to attend night school three evenings a week.

Having, with Mr Robinson's help, passed the necessary entrance certificate, I decided on the latter course.

My mother persuaded Mr Scholes to take me on as an apprentice and so I signed a Deed of Apprenticeship, in which I agreed to work hard, be faithful to my master and carry out all his reasonable bidding. For the first year I would receive the sum of five shillings a week, the second year, ten shillings and the third year, one pound a week.

When I started work, I found that Mr Scholes had another apprentice called Albert Martin.

Mr Scholes, in addition being an optician, was also a qualified chemist, although he didn't practise as such. His wife Elsie owned two chemists' shops in Hoylake, so we also had another optical practice over one of the chemist's shops.

Albert and I got on famously together. He spent most of his time at the Hoylake practice, whilst I was at West Kirby.

We were both expected each morning to open our premises, do any necessary floor polishing and dusting, open all the mail, check work from the prescription houses, book appointments, do any small repairs which came in, go debt collecting, and do anything else which turned up.

Three afternoons a week we were released from our duties and made our way to Manchester in time for the evening sessions at the university, which used to be from 6.00-9.30pm.

Getting there meant taking a bus to Birkenhead, then taking the underground railway to Liverpool and walking to Lime Street Station to get the steam train to Manchester. We used to arrive back home about midnight.

We did this irksome journey for a year and then Albert commandeered the family car. We split the running costs and used that for the remaining two years.

We generally arrived in Manchester at about 4.30pm, had a meal at the Waldorf Snack Bar, and then if there was any spare time, had a look around the second-hand car showrooms, dreaming of the day when we could buy a Jaguar.

Just before I left school, I had acquired a girlfriend. By that time I was 17 and a well-proportioned six-footer with an Austin Swallow (although it belonged to my mother).

I had briefly met one or two of the local girls, but I had been particularly attracted to a couple of dark-haired beauties whom I used to see rollerskating along the promenade and cavorting about in the open-air swimming pool.

One night I plucked up courage and got talking to them. They were two sisters, Marjorie and Nora. Marjorie was the younger and prettier of the two. Apparently they were each in charge of one of the local coal offices.

I suggested to Marjorie that perhaps she might like to go to the pictures with me. To my delight she agreed that she would.

The next night I picked her up and we went to the Gaumont Palace in Chester, which was a lovely new cinema with plush red seats and a Wurlitzer organ.

I realised that Marjorie must be older than me – but I am sure she had no idea that I was still going to school, or she would probably have ditched me.

This was every schoolboy's dream and I was 'over the moon'. Unfortunately my sister Mixie saw us out together at a tea shop in Mold and told my mother, who promptly cut off all my pocket money.

It was difficult to take a girl to the pictures if you hadn't got any money.

I used to get money each week to pay for my school dinners, so if I was going to hold on to Marjorie, I had no option – I had to forgo my dinners and exist on a tuppenny bun or a bag of crisps.

One day one of my buns contained a bonus in the shape of a full length bootlace complete with metal tag.

Eventually I left school and once I had started work I managed to scrounge a bit more pocket money.

It turned out that Marjorie was a Sunday school teacher, so I wasn't able to see her on Sunday afternoons; she did however compensate by taking me to church on a Sunday night.

The two sisters were very athletic and great swimmers. I used to feel a bit of a wimp when we went to the baths and they both climbed up to the top diving board.

They persuaded me that I ought to take up ice skating, so we all ended up going to the Ice Palace in Liverpool most Saturday nights in the winter.

We had great times together and had a steady relationship during the three years when I was going to the university.

There came the time when I qualified and began looking for a job.

When she knew that I would be leaving the district, Marjorie delivered me an ultimatum. Either we got engaged right away, or she would wish to end our relationship.

I was at a stage where I had just made the acquaintance of an attractive blonde at the university. And in addition, at this critical stage in my career, starting a new job and having no money, I didn't want to be tied down. So reluctantly we parted.

CHAPTER 6

EARLY YEARS

Having qualified as an ophthalmic optician in 1936 I immediately started looking for a job. Jobs were not easy to come by in 1936 and I wrote many letters before I finally received a reply. Would I kindly go for an interview? I put on my best suit and crossed the River Mersey to Liverpool.

The address I had been given was in London Road. I eagerly scanned the area, expecting 49a to be an optician's premises – however it appeared to be a dingy office over a grocer's shop.

I ascended the stairs and knocked on the door, entering when I was asked to 'come in". I was met by a seedy-looking girl who told me to take a seat, as Mr Goldstein was interviewing people for the job and would see me presently. Alarm bells began to ring. Before the war optics was in its infancy – it was not under any sort of government control and no qualifications were necessary to be called an optician.

I awaited my interview with interest. In due course the door opened and I was motioned to take a seat. The room was bare apart from a desk and two chairs, and a pile of small suitcases rested on the table. My interviewer was in his shirtsleeves and was about 50 years of age. He wore large black-rimmed glasses and had a foreign accent. He beckoned me to a seat and opened one of the suitcases. Inside there was a miniature trial case, a trial frame, a small reading chart and an assortment of cheap frames. He spoke: "Each day you will report here. We will make a series of appointments for you. We will pay you £2 a week plus commission. We will also pay all your bus fares and allow you 2s a day for your lunch. You will deposit the suitcase back here each night."

I was absolutely appalled.

I had heard about this sort of quackery but when actually being confronted with it, it was a different matter. I told our friend in no uncertain terms what I thought of him and his job. I certainly had not spent four years of hard study to attain the Fellowship of the British Optical Association in order to ply my job from door to door. Unfortunately this was not an isolated case of the quackery that was being practised at that time. It was many years before opticians were finally registered and it became illegal for unqualified people to carry out an eye examination.

A few weeks later I finally landed a proper job in Mansfield, a mining town in the centre of the Dukeries.

Whilst I was at the university and in my final year, I happened to drop in on a course which was just starting and there, seated at one of the benches in the laboratory, I saw a fantastic blue-eyed blonde. I could not believe my eyes. I made an excuse to speak to her and I was immediately a fallen man. All the girls on my course had thick Lancashire accents but this creature seemed to purr like a kitten. I could not sleep at night for thinking of her.

The firm for which I was going to work was the CWS. I had not really wanted to work for a multiple, but my main object at that time was to gain lots of experience before I opened my own practice. The CWS had its main offices in the city centre in Manchester. I would be working for the main body, but loaned out to the Mansfield CWS, an affiliated Society.

Before I took up my appointment in Mansfield I had to have two weeks training in Manchester, so I booked into the Deansgate Hotel and to my delight discovered that Sheila, my new heartthrob, lived in Sale, one of the suburbs. I rang her and invited her to a tea dance at the State Restaurant. My mother had provided me with a small car to enable me to take up my new job, so I was able to drive my new friend home. We met on several occasions during my stay in Manchester and it was with a heavy heart that I had to leave for Mansfield. Before I left I asked Sheila to marry me! She couldn't make me out and thought that I was 'bonkers'. She said that she had just finished with a boyfriend who had been too possessive and she did not want to be tied down. I promised to write and said that I would come up to Manchester to see her.

When I arrived in Mansfield it was late afternoon. I went along to the store and made the acquaintance of Jack Hayward, who I understood had been running the Optical Department for the past two years single-handed. Jack was about my age and a cheerful individual; we immediately gelled and got on very well together. It was too late to go hunting for accommodation so I spent the night in his digs. It is not easy getting suitable digs in a strange town and in the ensuing months I had to move three times. I finally came to rest in a comfortable big old house run by a spinster lady and her widowed mother. 'Twink' was a cheerful character and ran the establishment with great efficiency. There were three other lodgers – Steve who was a chartered surveyor, Rowland a bank cashier, and David who was a dental surgeon. In addition we occasionally used to have Reginald Dixon, the famous Blackpool organist staying when he was doing a guest appearance at the local cinema.

We all got on well together and used to have the occasional wild night out, doing all the pubs in Nottingham and finishing up at the Palais de Danse. Happy days with empty roads and no breathalizers! There was always a nice fire burning in the grate and a hot meal waiting for us in the evening. One night we were served up sausage and mash. During the week we seemed to have had a surfeit of sausages and, as it was not done to leave anything on our plates, we had deposited several unwanted sausages in the fire. Twink came in to serve our second course and moved over to the fire. "Eh, that fire looks a bit dead, I'll just give it a bit of a poke." She ended up with a sausage on the end of her poker. Nothing was said but we were all nearly bursting with laughter. Needless to say we were not given sausages again for a couple of weeks.

I soon found that I would realise my ambitions and get plenty of experience in my optics. At least 50 per cent of our patients were miners and so we would see many cases involving injuries and diseases endemic to the mining fraternity.

My weekly pay was £3 5s 0d and for that we worked non-stop from 9am until 7pm and on Fridays from 9am to 9pm. Wednesday was a half-day holiday and we finished at 12 noon. Mind you, £3 5s 0d in those days bought quite a lot. I kept writing to my blue-eyed blonde nearly every day and eagerly waited for a letter in return. The weeks went by without a word. I tried ringing up but she always seemed to be out. I began to despair and felt really wretched. One day just before the Easter holiday I got a phone call from her mother.

"You know, Sheila really likes you, but she has been so put off by the possessiveness of her late boy friend that she has been a bit reluctant to start a fresh relationship. I suggest that you ring her. She will be in at 7.30 this evening."

I would have two days' holiday at Easter, so I did ring that evening and asked if I could go over and see her. To my delight she said "yes". The next day I drove over to Sale, picked her up and we went to Southport for the day. We had tea at Rowntree's Restaurant and then went to the pictures. It was 10.30pm before – *bliss, oh bliss* – we embraced for the first time and I started on my long drive back to Mansfield. This was the start of our love affair and from then on there was no keeping me away from Sale. I used to drive over to Manchester on Wednesday afternoons, my half-day holiday. We would have a 1s 6d steak and chips at the Waldorf Restaurant and then go ice skating. I would then land back in Mansfield at 1am. Some weeks the hedgerows were packed five feet high with snow but I somehow managed to get through. Later on, when we became engaged, Sheila's mother took pity on me, so I also used to go over when I finished work on a Saturday night, stay the night and leave for the return to Mansfield at six on Monday morning.

CHAPTER 7

TIME TO MOVE ON

After working for a year and a half in Mansfield I considered that I now had sufficient experience to open my own practice, so I gave in my notice. I managed to scrape together £500 as my total capital. The thing was, where to start? I was now living at home in Birkenhead with my widowed mother and her spinster sister. Where would be the best place to start a practice? I visited the local library and began to work out statistics. I even thought of places as far away as Bristol but eventually it turned out that Ellesmere Port had the highest birth rate and lowest unemployment figures for the whole country. This at least sounded promising, and had the added advantage that it was close to Birkenhead. I would be able to commute from home.

On a cold winter's day I drove over to spy out the land. At that time Ellesmere Port was split into two halves by a railway crossing. There was also a subterranean tunnel on one side called the Cattle Arch, where cattle used to be driven through. There was the new end of the town, where all the better shops were situated, and the other side of the crossing was the Port End, where there were what looked like a straggling conglomerate of Army and Navy stores and the usual cheap clothes and boot shops. Moving further out of the town I discovered that there was a thriving dock area where ships from overseas would discharge timber, cattle food and all sorts of other commodities. Also at this end of the town there was the Manchester Ship Canal where large barges were being loaded with goods for transit to all parts of the country. In addition there was an enormous flour mill and a large ironworks. I was beginning to think that the town had possibilities. Further investigation revealed that there were a number of engineering firms and the vast Shell oil refinery.

The town itself at that time was certainly not very inspiring -- it was ill-lit and scruffy. It was obviously trying its best to cater for the rapidly increasing population but was being torn apart by the awful railway crossing – which had to be closed constantly to allow trains bound for Hooton or Helsby to pass through.

There was not a premises of any kind to let in the better part of the town and I began to despair. Eventually, in the dockside end of the town, I espied a shop which had been divided into two. The left half was occupied by a barber's. The right half was empty and had a 'To Let' notice in the window. I popped into the barber shop to enquire where I could get a key to carry out an inspection. Apparently it was owned by a local building firm, whose premises were close by. Having got the key I opened the door and looked in, only to discover that the ground floor was impossibly small for my purpose. There was an open space with a staircase on the right hand side. Upstairs I found that there was an enormous room with windows which went right down to the floor. There was also another small room, down two steps. I thought that the upstairs could be suitably converted into a consulting room, an office and a waiting room. The only trouble was that the stairs would be a serious disadvantage, particularly to the elderly who constitute about 75 per cent of our patients. It was obviously the wrong side of town, but in a cul-de-sac right opposite were the local cinema, the library and the Alhambra Ballroom.

I decided there and then that it was worth taking a chance. I went to see the builder who agreed for a nominal charge to divide up the top room to my requirements. The next step was a trip to London to order all the equipment I should require for my new consulting room. Whilst I was waiting for delivery, I busied myself decorating the premises. I visited the local saleroom and on the auction day acquired six dining room chairs, a large Indian carpet, a roll-top desk and a deck chair! I did not attempt to furnish the office, as of course my funds were being stretched to the limit. My mother kindly made me a net curtain for the window, to provide privacy, as my office consisted of a roll-top desk, bare boards and a deck chair. The latter was used a good deal in the first few months whilst I was anxiously waiting for patients to arrive.

My dining chairs, six pictures scrounged from home and a small table piled with magazines completed my waiting room. The small back room I rigged out as a workshop. Starting a new practice in a strange town where you do not know a soul, and have only a small amount of capital, can be a very harrowing experience. Back in 1937, optics was an uncontrolled profession and unqualified quacks were everywhere. There were the 'door to door merchants' that I've mentioned before, Woolworths' ready-made spectacles and even so-called 'Indian eye specialists' who would cure any known eye disease for £1 – so I realised I was going to have an uphill struggle to get established.

The day came for my grand opening! Obviously I could not afford a cleaner or a receptionist, so I arrived early, lit the tiny coke-fired central heating stove, washed the stairs, and then sat down in my deck chair and waited for the door bell to ring downstairs. I should explain that, not having a receptionist, I had painted at the bottom of the stairs a hand pointing upwards, and underneath 'PLEASE COME UPSTAIRS.'

Nothing happened for the first four days. Oh dear, was I going to go bankrupt? Then on the Friday the bell eventually rang. By this time, having spent the entire week reading and playing darts, I was feeling distinctly apprehensive. I counted the footsteps as the unknown stranger mounted the stairs. It turned out to be a middle-aged lady. She told me that she was glad to see that at last there was a properly qualified optician in the town. Would I examine her eyes, as she was experiencing difficulty with her reading?

I ushered her into the consulting room – and so started a practice, which now, over 60 years later, has been taken over by my son.

Whilst I was trying to get my practice going, Sheila was still getting on quietly with her studies. As she was free on a Saturday, she used to come over to Ellesmere Port and keep me company. When I finished at 6pm we would go into Chester and have a few drinks before going back to her home in Sale, where we could spend all day Sunday together.

The practice was hard going for the first few months, but gradually people started to drift in and I began to make a profit – not a large one, but sufficient to enable us to get married. We finally arranged our wedding for August 25th, 1939, which turned out to be the week before war broke out. Our honeymoon consisted of a weekend at Llanbedr. Not much, but in view of the war news, we were anxious to get back to sort out our little home and prepare for an unknown future.

By this time Sheila had finished her course and was a fully qualified optician. There was obviously as yet not sufficient business to keep two opticians busy, so she became my part-time assistant and meanwhile occupied herself in the home and garden. It would have been possible for her to have got a job working for another firm, but the war clouds were looming, so I felt that she ought to be gradually integrated into our own practice, and therefore get loads of practical experience so that she could take over when I inevitably had to join the army.

CHAPTER 8

WAR CLOUDS GATHER

It was a bitter-sweet part of our lives. We were so much in love and were deliriously happy – if only this could have gone on for ever – but we knew that our time together would be short, so we made the most of it. The days raced by into ten precious months and then on July 8th, 1940 my calling-up notice arrived. The bottom dropped out of our world. The awful unknown had arrived. Where would I be posted? When would we see each other again?

I was sent down to the Royal Military Academy at Woolwich for my basic training. It had been decided by the powers-that-be that all opticians would be drafted into the Royal Electrical and Mechanical Engineers. In view of their optical knowledge, they would be trained in engineering, with a view to servicing all the optical instruments which the Army uses, such as binoculars, dial sights, rangefinders, theodolites, tank instruments, etc. After an intensive six-months course and numerous exams, we were classified as instrument mechanics 1st class and were ready for posting – to a disused lace factory in Nottingham. We had not got a clue as to where we might be going but one day we were paraded to the quartermaster's store and kitted out with 'topees' and other tropical kit, so we knew that we were not going to Iceland – but that was all. Security was very tight, and even when we were embarked on our ships, we did not know where we were bound for. We were told that we would be given a day's leave in order to say goodbye to our loved ones. I phoned my darling wife with the dreaded news. She closed the practice, drove over to Nottingham and booked us a room at the Welbeck Hotel. It was not a happy day as we both felt wretched. That night as we lay in each other's arms, the tears began to fall. We clung to each other in desperation, praying that the dawn would never come. Unfortunately it did, and the next morning came the dreadful moment of parting. As we embraced with our last frantic kisses and said goodbye, we knew not when we would be together again.

We paraded at midnight the next day and marched to the station a mile away in the pouring rain. An hour later a blacked-out train steamed in. We scrambled into a carriage in the pitch dark and wondered where we were bound for.

In the early morning, after many stops, we finally trundled into Liverpool. Army trucks arrived and deposited us on the dockside where we sat on our kitbags in the perishing cold until 6pm when we were finally allowed to board our liner, the *Strathallan*. Life in the hold of a troopship as a private was not to be recommended. Officers and NCOs were all accommodated in cabins on the upper decks and even had the use of the swimming pool. Our accommodation consisted of rows of narrow tables with a bench on either side. There were ten men to each table. At the end of the tables, there was a bench under which all our plates and cups were stored. Over the tables, there was a long shelf on which our kitbags, steel helmets, gas masks and so on had to be neatly stood. Each night, two men from each table were detailed to go down into the bowels of the ship to bring up the hammocks on which we were strung up at night. It meant five journeys into the hold. For the first week after we sailed, we had to sleep in our battle-dresses and with our boots on in case we were torpedoed. (The *Strathallan* was torpedoed and sunk when on a later convoy.) If you required to get to the latrine in the middle of the night, it was necessary to crawl underneath a sea of hammocks avoiding if possible the offerings of your seasick mates.

Fresh water was in short supply and so the taps were turned on for two short periods each day, during which time you had to wash either your shirt or your body. The food with which we were dished up was mostly porridge with no sugar or milk, stew, and rice without milk or sugar. There was a canteen where it was possible to buy small tins of condensed milk, but as we had not received any pay, this was only for the prudent ones who still had a few shillings left. When we got into the tropics, the heat was so bad down below that we were allowed to forgo the luxury of our hammocks if we wished and go up to the next deck, which was above the waterline, and sleep on any bit of floor that we could find. It was heaven to get away from the heat and stench below.

The one bright spot on the voyage was when we called in at Cape Town for two days. It was a wonderful sight that greeted us as we sailed into the harbour. The entire town was ablaze with light and the whole of our massive convoy also had its lights on. We were allowed shore leave for the two days that we were there. We were like canaries let out of their cages and we certainly made the most of our freedom. The shops were full of all sorts of tempting items, such as great mounds of oranges, bananas and other fruits, which of course we had not seen in England for ages. We had very little money between us to take advantage of these luxuries. But Eric Piper, my mate, and I were fortunate. We were looking in a shop window, when a big black sedan drew up. A middle-aged gentleman got out and came across.

"Hello, lads – glad to welcome you to our city. Have you got anything arranged for the day?"

"No, we have not, we have only just arrived."

"That's great, then. I want you to be my guests for the day."

We scrambled into the car and, before we had really got our bearings, arrived at a lovely big villa on the side of a mountain. It transpired that our benefactor was a dental surgeon and had taken the day off work especially to entertain the troops on their short stay. We were introduced to his wife and his beautiful daughter, who was apparently training to be a ballet dancer. We had glasses of wine thrust into our hands and spent the next hour having our glasses refilled. We then sat down to a superb lunch. After lunch we were joined by the family in the car and were taken on a tour of the beauty spots. Later on we went to a 'super dooper' night club called the 'Del Monica' which had a ceiling resembling the sky at night, with a moon and twinkling stars. After a show and a superb dinner, we were bundled into the car again and whisked right up to the top of Table Mountain, where we could enjoy the magnificent panorama of lights below. We were then taken on a little further, to an outside café where the waiters came out, fixed trays to the car windows, and then brought us coffee and biscuits. Finally, at midnight we were driven back to our ship. We could not believe how lucky we had been, but apparently we were not the only ones. The South Africans were very generous people and they made a big thing of welcoming troops on their way to the Middle East. We were indeed sorry to be leaving this beautiful country and its wonderful hospitality. As we sailed away for the remainder of our long voyage, the lone and haunting figure of the 'White Lady' gradually disappeared into the mist. 'The White Lady of Cape Town' was a famous lady who, wrapped in a white veil, stood right at the end of the pier and sang a farewell as the troopships left harbour.

 The weather got hotter and hotter as we approached the Red Sea, and we were eventually allowed to change into our tropical kit. After seven weeks we arrived in Suez. The temperature was well over 100°F. There was a train alongside the harbour. Before we boarded the train, we decided that it was time to wash some of the sweat off our burning backs, so it was off with all our clothes and straight into the sea, which was like a warm bath. It was a couple of hours before the train was due to leave, so we had a real good wallow. The train was very slow and uncomfortable – it had plain wooden seats and no windows. It stopped at a number of little stations, which during the night were lit by flaming torches. The crowds of souvenir hawkers and beggars we passed by didn't give us much chance of a doze. We finally arrived in Cairo about midnight and were transported by trucks to the transport barracks within the Citadel. I remained there until my first posting, which was to the 9th Heavy AA Regt, which was responsible for the air defence of Alexandria. I was posted to many different parts of Egypt and Palestine but eventually ended up at a soul-destroying base camp called Tel el Kebir. It was an enormous depot surrounded by guards and barbed wire – out in the desert, miles from civilisation – and was the service depot which backed up the 8th Army. All the damaged tanks, motor vehicles, wireless equipment and scientific instruments were sent back there for repair and reconditioning.

Our Instrument Shop was a quarter of a mile across the desert from the camp in which we lived in tents, eight men to a tent. At 7am each day we paraded in full gear, including our rifles, and marched to work across the desert; we then marched back for lunch and then back to work until 6pm. Our instrument workshop was hermetically sealed to keep out the dust and had no air conditioning, so in summer was stiflingly hot. The work was interesting but precise and very tiring. Trying to clean the graticules and centre prism system of a rangefinder in a temperature of 95°F with sweat pouring down your legs, could try the patience of a saint.

The powers-that-be decided that I was a suitable candidate for an Arm. Art. Staff Sergeant's course, so I collected my kit and was bundled off back to school. We were on trial for a month and were given the rank of corporal. The first month was hell, with exams every week. It consisted of tests in algebra, geometry, trigonometry, hydrostatics and mechanics. We then went on to desert navigation and army procedures, and had an intricate trade test on filing eight pieces of brass and steel. The outdoor part of the course included firing a rifle, Bren gun and pistol on the range and, finally, taking charge of a squad on the square and putting them through all the rifle and other drills in front of the RSM. If you failed the first month's assessment, your stripes came down and you were sent back to your unit. If you passed after the first month, you became an acting Sergeant and started on the course proper, which lasted about four months, with an exam each week. At the end of the course, if successful, you added a crown above your three stripes and became a Staff Sergeant. The jump from Private to Staff Sergeant took a bit of getting used to at first. It was a highly-responsible position and I quickly found that I was the guy who made things work. The officers did all the paper work and issued orders, but the Staff Sergeant was the one who had to organise and deliver the goods. Life immediately became more tolerable. The Sergeants' Mess was an oasis of comfort with a well-stocked bar, a dining tent with tablecloths on the tables and Egyptian waiters in snow-white *galabias* adorned with the regimental flash.

Eventually, after four years abroad, I received an order saying that I was to be repatriated on compassionate grounds. My mother had been ill with cancer for some time and her doctor had applied for my repatriation. It was 1945 and the war in Europe was nearly over, so we did not have to go round the Cape this time. I arrived back in Gourock, Scotland. On disembarking, we found ourselves in a church hall. We were told that there were beds for the night in the barracks which was over a mile away, or if we did not feel like walking that far, we could sleep on the hall floor where we were. We decided to doss down on our one blanket which we carried in our kitbags and covered ourselves with our greatcoats. The next morning we were up bright and early, were issued with our travel warrants, and in my case I got straight on the train for Liverpool, then the underground railway to Birkenhead and finally a bus which luckily dropped me right outside my front door in Whitby, Ellesmere Port. I dumped my kitbag and rifle in the porch and rang the bell. The door immediately sprang open and there was my own gorgeous blue-eyed blonde, bringing to life the misty vision that I had carried in my mind for the last four years. What heaven it was to hold her in my arms once again.

CHAPTER 9

START OF A NEW LIFE (BROOK HOUSE)

During the war Sheila had been running our optical practice very successfully, she – clever thing – had even managed to move to the better end of the town. Business had immediately doubled.

It took three or four days to arrange, as she now had a busy practice, but we decided that we ought to have a holiday to celebrate my return, so we put a notice on the door 'CLOSED FOR A WEEK'.

During the war years Sheila had acquired an ancient tandem which she used to ride with a girlfriend. We decided that we would use this and do a tour of North Wales. It was early spring and the weather wasn't kind; it rained most of the time, but we were so engrossed with our love for each other that we never even noticed it. That is, apart from stripping off each night and drying our sodden clothes in front of the hotel's electric stove. We set off each morning at about nine and usually covered about 50 miles a day, although on one memorable occasion on the way home we did more than 100 miles. This was a time of course when petrol was rationed and roads were relatively traffic-free.

START OF A NEW LIFE (BROOK HOUSE)

At the end of my leave I was posted to Oswestry. The war was over and I couldn't believe how 'cushy' it was there. I had my own little room, complete with fireplace. There were lovely hot showers and a super Sergeants' Mess with log fires, dining tables with tablecloths and white-uniformed ATS waiters.

During the short time that I was at Oswestry, Sheila and I used to commute on a Wednesday evening to meet at Wrexham. She would cycle from Ellesmere Port and I would cycle from Oswestry. We then had dinner at the Wynnstay Arms in Wrexham. After a few months my discharge papers came through. Following a medical examination, I handed in all my army gear, collected my free suit and was once again a free man. After a few days at home I returned to my rightful place in the practice and Sheila had a well-earned rest.

My mother had cancer and had been seriously ill for two years. She had received all the treatment which was available at that time. When the Good Lord finally took her, we felt that it was a merciful release. In her will she left me a row of six houses in Walton in Liverpool. They were all let at 13s 6d a week each and the landlord was responsible for all the repairs. I used to go there on a Wednesday afternoon with a bag of tools in the back of my car. I would collect the rents, mark off the tenants' rent books and then carry out the various minor repairs which always seemed to be necessary. After a while, major repairs like burst boilers and cracked WC cisterns started to make it appear that I was flogging a dead horse. I could earn far more money by staying at home and doing a couple of extra hours in my optical practice.

The houses that I had inherited were excellent and in a good district opposite a park, but in those days of restricted tenancy it was impossible to raise the rents, so they became an uneconomical investment. I decided to sell. I put them in the hands of an estate agent and they were bought by a large firm who, I understood, would be up to all sorts of tricks to obtain vacant possession, when the properties would be much more valuable. Today of course, they would be worth a small fortune

Having now acquired a respectable sum of capital, and with a thriving practice, we decided to go house-hunting for a home of our own. We both felt that we would like to get away from the claustrophobia of Ellesmere Port and acquire a home in the country. We went to all the estate agents, read all the local newspapers and then went out in the car and scoured the area within a 15-mile radius. We eventually saw a country estate of 14½ acres at Huxley, a village about 15 miles away, near to Beeston and Peckforton castles. It was advertised at £7,000 and had a lodge at its gate which was available for £2,000. Ridiculous – we could not possibly afford that! But anyhow we decided that as it was a nice day, we would go and look. The lodge, which was adjoining the driveway to the house, was charming. It was in the Tudor style and had an 'olde worlde' garden. We were given to understand that it was let to a retired doctor and his wife. We drove up the rhododendron-lined drive in our little Standard 8 and arrived on a large circular gravel forecourt.

To our eyes the house looked magnificent. It was double bow-fronted, three storeys high and had an observatory on the top. We climbed the sandstone steps up to the impressive front door and raised the enormous brass hand which served as a knocker. We waited in the wisteria-lined porch with trepidation. We were greeted by an attractive lady, who was obviously of the 'County Set.' She told us that she was divorced and was remarrying, so therefore wished to sell. We were given a conducted tour of the premises and found that it encompassed six bedrooms (two en-suite), three entertaining rooms, a large kitchen with an Aga, a butler's pantry, scullery and saddle room. But we had hardly started yet. There were enormous wine cellars, with a hatch to roll the barrels down, a conservatory which was badly in need of repair, and a 40ft-long annexe which had been used by one of the previous owners as a Sunday School for the local children.

When we were taken to the back door, we descended into a cobbled courtyard, which contained a garage and loose boxes with a hay barn over them. Outside the courtyard there was an enormous T-shaped building in which rested a large horse carriage. Next door was a room for the groom, with its own fireplace. There was also a further barn and hound kennels.

We were enthralled – but it was crazy, of course. It was much too big for our few pitiful possessions. We went home and talked until the small hours. We had by this time got a one-month-old daughter, and felt that some time in the not too distant future she should have a brother and sister, so thinking ahead, we would probably be able to occupy some of the space. This was immediately after a long war, when people hadn't really recovered and property sales were in depression.

We decided to put in an offer quite a bit lower than the asking price with a 'deadline' of two days. To our amazement and delight our offer was accepted and we were now the proud owners of a country estate. When the day for removal arrived, the entire belongings from our little rented Whitby house occupied about half of the 30ft x 7ft hall.

It caused us much amusement when the coalman arrived for an order and, looking down the hall, said he hoped the rest of our furniture would be arriving shortly.

The house had been somewhat neglected – it wanted completely redecorating and one of the bathrooms needed re-tiling. I decided to commandeer the butler's pantry as a workshop and spent all my spare time during the next six months decorating and doing running repairs.

CHAPTER 10

RIDING ADVENTURES

After moving into Brook House, which was in the heart of the Cheshire hunting country, we decided that we ought to brush up on our riding. We had each of us had a few riding lessons, but had still got a lot to learn. We enrolled with the George Oldfield School of Riding and were very soon 'horsebound'.

Sheila was very taken with an Irish confidential hunter of 15.3hh called Kerry. George wasn't very keen on selling her as Kerry was the most sought-after ride in his stables. Anyway, I made him an offer he couldn't refuse and we became the proud owners of our first hunter.

We shared Kerry for the first six months whilst we were trying to improve our riding technique, but then found that it was a bit lonely going out for a ride by yourself, so I started looking for a mount of my own.

One day reading through the local rag I saw an advert offering a grey cob gelding for sale.

We went to investigate, had a trial ride and bought him.

We brought Joss home and with some trepidation put him in the same field as Kerry, praying that they would settle down together. For the first half hour she chased him round and round the field and did her best to bite a piece out of his backside. They eventually settled down and became good friends.

The only snag about having a mare and a gelding together is that it's a hell of a job to get the gelding to leave the mare and go out hacking on his own.

I soon found that Joss had a bad fault – he was scared stiff of cattle lorries.

I had gone out for a ride on my own. We were on a quiet country lane not far from home, and glancing around I suddenly I realised that the local bus was behind us. Joss whinnied in fright and started to canter. I tried to calm him down but it was no use – he got the bit between his teeth and broke into a headlong gallop. My frantic tugging on the reins hadn't the slightest effect. Sparks shot from his hooves as we tore down the lane. I'm sure he thought all the devils were behind him.

The idiot who was driving the bus, instead of slowing down, came closer and closer and started sounding his horn. In those days crash hats weren't worn and the road beneath Joss's hooves looked very hard indeed. Fortunately we eventually came to a side road which I managed to divert him down, but it took another half mile before he slowed down and became manageable.

The second incident was even more serious. I was once again on my own, enjoying a ride near Peckforton Castle. Suddenly Joss pricked up his ears, a sure sign that he was getting nervous. When I looked round, there, sure enough, was a large cattle lorry following us. There was a wide grass verge to the left, so I eased him over, off the road, hoping that he would settle down. Not a bit of it. He snorted in terror and broke into a gallop. Ahead of us was a telegraph pole with a galvanised wire support. In his panic he headed straight for it. Mental images of decapitation flashed before my eyes. At the last moment I managed to drag his head to one side, but his shoulder hit the pole with a bang and nearly uprooted it. The force of the impact brought him down on his knees and I jumped off, thanking my Maker for a miraculous escape. Joss shook his head and scrambled to his feet. Apparently none the worse for the accident, he took off down the lane. He gradually calmed down and started to graze on a nice green patch 200 yards away. With the aid of an apple, which I always kept in my pocket, I managed to recapture him and rode him home.

On another occasion, Sheila had taken him to the local blacksmith to be shod.

"It's all right, Mrs Orrell, you needn't worry, I'll bring him home."

"Well, make sure that you come the back way – it's a bit further but he doesn't like cattle lorries."

Henry, the blacksmith, apparently did not heed this advice. Joss arrived home on his own, covered in sweat, having deposited Henry in the nearest ditch.

We eventually decided that Joss was a dangerous liability, so we rang up a horse dealer to see if he would be interested in a part exchange.

Yes – he had got a beautiful 16.1hh bay gelding with no vices whatsoever, and he would bring him round for our inspection!

A beautiful horsebox drove into the yard and we waited impatiently for first sight of this wonder horse. George Hall, the dealer, was quite a character and he certainly knew his horseflesh. He lowered the door of his wagon, and slowly backed out Ventry. He was, indeed, an impressive-looking animal. He had been groomed to perfection, his coat gleamed, and his mane and long tail had even been plaited. George ran him backwards and forwards across the yard and then, as a *pièce de resistance* halted him in front of us and yelled 'HUP' wherepon Ventry obediently lifted each of his feet in turn for inspection. Sheila and I looked at each other. Yes! This was class – we were sold.

What about a part-exchange? George in the manner of dealers, pursed his lips and blew his nose, and looked at Joss.

Joss, of course, being a hunting cob was a heavier build, and in the manner of cobs had a bobbed tail. Against the elegant Ventry he looked a bit of a ragamuffin.

"Well, of course you couldn't ride him, you could put him in a milk float or something like that."

After the usual argy-bargy a deal was eventually struck and we said goodbye to Joss. There was an amusing sequel. Some months afterwards, we were visiting some friends in Heswall. They had a daughter who was a member of a pony club. She had just returned from a gymkhana where all the competitors were apparently scared stiff of a grey cob which was rumoured to be a very good jumper. Guess what! That's right – it was our old friend Joss.

Ventry proved to be completely traffic-proof, a beautiful ride and altogether a more enjoyable companion.

When we first arrived at Brook House we found that there was an old orchard in one of the fields at the front of the house. In the manner of old orchards, you occasionally get a bumper crop. It so happened that luckily this was just such a year.

There were about twenty 15ft-high apple and pear trees, which were showering down their bounty. Fresh fruit was still much sought-after, so I arranged with a greengrocer in Whitby to take delivery of a couple of sacks a day. We also had a legacy of a number of rows of beetroot which the previous owner had planted. It seemed a pity to waste them, particularly as we had a large Aga cooker, so a large pan of beetroot was kept boiling every day. On my way to work I dropped off any surplus produce we had, until supplies ran out. It was a welcome addition to the coffers and enabled us to purchase all the necessary items required for our renovations.

Having 14½ acres of land we had to decide what to do with it. We started off by letting eight acres to the farmer next door. The remainder, with the exception of the pleasure gardens which covered about two acres, we kept as pasture for our two hunters. Oh! I forgot, we did keep half an acre for a mad-brained fruit-growing enterprise.

Flushed with the success of our apple and pear sales, we decided that we would start to grow soft fruit.

I bought a Clifford Rotary Cultivator and spent all my spare time working on the half acre. Having worked up a suitable tilth, I started to plant it out with long rows of strawberries, raspberries and blackcurrants. They looked most impressive and I had visions of piles of lucrative soft fruit to sell.

Word quickly got about that we had a glut of strawberries. Mrs Thompson, one of our farming neighbours, arrived one Sunday afternoon, ostensibly on a social visit:

"Oh, what a lovely lot of strawberries!"

"Yes, Mrs Thompson they are, aren't they! Would you like to swop for some cream?"

Sheila filled a big basket with strawberries and our neighbour departed. We saw no more of her for a fortnight, until one evening Sheila excitedly called out to me: "Mrs Thomson is coming up the drive. I expect she has brought our cream."

After half an hour of gossip, a small carton containing half a pound of blackcurrants was produced.

"I just brought you these, Mrs Orrell – I picked them in my daughter's garden this morning."

Farmers, as a breed, are notoriously tardy with their favours. A few months afterwards, when Sheila was confined to bed, having just given birth to our son Richard, Mrs Thomson knocked on the front door. She had a large wicker basket on her arm and had come to see the baby. I led her upstairs and sat her down on a chair by the bedside. She fumbled in her basket and started to unwrap a large piece of cheese which she then presented to Sheila. The Thomsons were one of the largest cheese producers in the area, and so I thought, "What a nice gesture." However, having already experienced farming generosity, I thought that I had better query it.

"That's a nice piece of cheese, Mrs Thompson. What do I owe you for it?"

"Well, Mr Orrell, I did just pop it on the scales before I came out and it came to 2s 6d.'"

Being completely inexperienced I didn't realise how quickly weeds could grow. In no time at all, our rows of soft fruit were smothered in weeds and docks 2ft high. I did my best to hoe them down but within a few days they were up as strong as ever. As the fruit ripened we were plagued by dozens of sparrows and blackbirds, which proceeded to strip the branches clean.

I just hadn't got the time to erect nets and do all the cultivation required, as the pleasure gardens and pathways were taking an awful lot of maintenance. I decided to market whatever we could and then abandon soft fruit growing.

My wife's parents were retired and lived in Surrey on a smallholding. At Easter we decided to pay them a visit for four days. Whilst we were down there we met their friends who had a small herd of Jersey cows.

"Why not have a house cow and produce our own cream?" we wondered. Being impulsive people we bought a Jersey heifer and had her brought up to Cheshire.

When we bought Brook House we also 'took over' Sinclair – one of the old family retainer types. He was lean and wiry, about 40 years of age. He always wore brown corduroy trousers, black boots, a dark grey woollen waistcoat with a watch chain across and a cap which he proceeded to touch every time he greeted you. And, oh yes, he always wore a stiff white winged collar.

Sinclair was quite a character. He "had always worked for gentlemen", so he told me. He lived about 500 yards up the road on a smallholding which he shared with his brother. They ran four Red Poll cattle and sold milk.

Sinclair used to come in and work for us every morning. He would groom the hunters, garden and do any odd jobs which were necessary. He readily agreed to milk Josephine night and morning.

Having our own cow, we decided we should have a few hens, to become more self-sufficient.

Not knowing the first thing about hens, I went to Beeston Market and bought a dozen Black Leghorns. Sinclair hooted with laughter when he saw them.

"You'll no get many eggs out o' that lot!"

I must admit that when I got them home they looked like a lot of black crows. They were rarely on the ground, and rather than go into their house at night they would roost high up in the trees.

One day one of them became crop bound, which means that their crop swells up with corn – what to do with it? According to Sinclair the only thing was to kill it. This sounded a bit drastic, so I got out my poultry manual. According to them you could effect a cure by slitting open the sac and emptying out the corn. There was nothing to lose, so I decided to give it a try.

I got Sheila to hold the bird whilst I wielded a razor blade. I then proceeded to cut open the sac and started to empty the seed out with a teaspoon. The bird was not in the least perturbed and was even trying to eat back the seed as I was spooning it out. Once the sac was empty I proceeded to sew it up with cotton. It survived, and was one of the few that ever laid.

They were not a great success, and as they gradually died off one by one, they were replaced by Light Sussex.

Our next project was geese to fatten for the Christmas trade. We bought a dozen goslings from one of the local farmers. We used to stretch some netting across to hold them in so that they would graze a patch at a time. At dusk we would bring them in to one of the stables and give them a hot meal. It was quite a sight of an evening to see them take to the air as one and fly up from the orchard for their supper.

After we had had Josephine for about six months and were revelling in lashings of cream and butter, I suddenly thought, "We have got this land which we are presently letting to a local farmer, why not make use of it ourselves?"

At that time (1948) the government was trying to eradicate tuberculosis in the country. A lot of cattle had no proper supply of drinking water. They were simply unchained from their stalls and sent out to drink from unfenced ponds, where of course they deposited their own dung. This gave rise to all sorts of diseases, including Johnne's disease and tuberculosis.

We had got one cow which was tuberculosis-free, so why not alter some of the loose boxes and get five more, starting a small attested herd?

The first thing was to find out what it would entail. I got in touch with the War Agricultural Committee, and in due course an official came and inspected the premises.

"Yes, the loose boxes could fairly easily be knocked down and partitioned off with galvanised stanchions. An automatic water bowl would have to be installed for each cow."

First snag. We had a plentiful water supply, but it originated from our own bore hole. We would need to have the water analysed to ensure that it was fit for TT cattle to drink. Apparently many farmers at that time had their applications turned down because their water was unfit for cattle consumption, although they themselves had been drinking it all their lives. They must have built up some sort of immunity!

The experts duly arrived and took samples of our water; we got the official results in a month's time. To our great relief it had passed all the tests. In addition to all the individual water bowls in the shippon, a piped water supply had to be available in all the fields where the cattle would be grazing. Also, as we were the only ones in the district to be going TT, all our fields would have to be double-fenced, to prevent our cattle from coming into contact with possible reactors. There did not seem to be any more insurmountable conditions, so we decided to go ahead. We contacted a local builder who soon changed the loose boxes into an ideal little shippon.

The next thing required was a dairy. In the yard close to the shippon there was an old wash-house which we no longer needed, so we gutted that and installed a milk cooler and steam sterilising plant. We now had a dairy.

Whilst the building work was going on, I had been cogitating on what breed of cattle to buy. I contacted Reg Roberts of Tarvin, who was generally recognised as an honest cattle dealer. He strongly advised me to have Ayrshires, a Scottish brown and white breed which were renowned for being 'good doers' with a high butterfat yield. They were also known for their resistance to TB. On Reg's advice, I ordered five in-calf Ayrshire heifers, straight down from the Scottish Highlands. When they arrived, I discovered that two of them had been calved for a week, so between them and Josephine, we were able to start TT milk production. The others would calve down in the next two or three days. Four days later we had an additional three mouths to feed – two heifers and one bull calf. We made a cosy partition in one of the barns and installed the calves in that.

True to his word, Sinclair turned up night and morning and ministered to the needs of our small herd. We had realised our ambition, and were now producing and marketing quality TT milk. Six cows were obviously not going to make a fortune but they provided the nucleus of a farming experience.

I became really interested in my little herd and avidly read all the agricultural books that I could lay my hands on. One day I was looking through the local paper and noticed that there was a one-day-a-week agricultural course starting in Whitchurch. I decided that I would attend.

It was extremely comprehensive for a one-day-a-week course. The mornings were given over to soil management and testing, also to learning about all the types of grasses and cereals, and the composition and use of fertilisers. The afternoon sessions dealt with all aspects of animal husbandry, including many tips on veterinary matters and dealing with injuries.

I bought a Ferguson tractor and cart, a plough and one or two other implements. Having read the appropriate book, I decided to plough up one of the fields and re-seed it. My ploughing would not have won a competition, but the seed prospered and in due course I had an excellent field of Italian Ryegrass, with the prospect of two crops of hay a year.

Besides our two hunters and cows, we also had a tortoiseshell cat called Tinker, who seemed always to be in an 'interesting condition' and setting us the task of finding homes for her progeny. Lassie, our pedigree Staffordshire Bull Terrier, could also be a bit of a worry. She was very socially minded and delighted in wandering around the district on her own. We were always being phoned by neighbours, to say that Lassie was sitting in front of their fire, and could we pick her up? She also had quite a retinue of suitors.

One night we heard a peculiar tapping on the front door. When we opened it, a gigantic lurcher shot past us down the passage and out through the back door. We began to think that it might steady her down if she had a family to look after, so we mated her with a suitably pedigreed male.

When her time came she presented us with eight adorable Staffordshire Bull Terriers.

I say 'adorable', but by the time they were eight weeks old they were a real crowd of toughies and used to knock hell out of each other. We decided to keep one of the males ourselves and christened him 'Lad'. We gave another one to a chemist friend of mine who fed her on all the patent baby foods, beef extracts etc. in his shop. She turned into a magnificent specimen but unfortunately inherited her mother's wanderlust. This left us with six more pups to dispose of.

We put an advert in the county newspaper and we had a number of enquiries, including a phone call from a very posh-sounding lady living in London. She would very much like to have a pup, but she lived in a luxury flat in Grosvenor Square which was full of antiques and Persian carpets. She would pay for the pup now, on condition that we would keep it for another few weeks and house-train it. We agreed to do as she asked, and when we were confident that we had fulfilled our part of the bargain we arranged with the buyer to send him by train to be met in London. We packed him in a crate with a supply of food and water and took him down to the station. We handed him over to the friendly guard on a train bound for London.

The next day a very angry Mrs Hope Robinson was on the phone. "The pup was not house-trained at all." When she had got him out of the crate, he had promptly emptied his bladder on one of her priceless rugs and ruined it. Her butler had also threatened to tender his notice. What did she expect the poor little thing to do? It would obviously take him a day or two to settle down after a stressful journey. I could see that there was no point in arguing, so I told her to send him back again and I would refund half of her purchase money.

He came back home the next day and I met him at the station. We eventually found him a very comfortable home with a local spinster.

Contrary to general opinion, Staffordshire Bull Terriers are not troublemakers and are the gentlest of dogs with young children. Our youngsters used to lie all over them and I never once heard a snap or growl.

When Lad grew up I used to take him with me when I went on my early morning ride. I would rise at 6am, saddle up, and go for an early morning hack around the neighbouring farms. All the farm dogs and mongrels used to bark and make a great show as we passed. Lad would take a wide berth to avoid any trouble and I used to feel rather ashamed of him. I knew he could just not be bothered. He would never attack unless provoked, but woe betide any cur that took a fancy to Lassie his mother – he would get them down and half-kill them unless I called him off.

Our first Christmas at Brook House was like something out of a Christmas carol. It was snowing on Christmas Eve and all the trees up the driveway were covered with fine powdered snowflakes. Our large open porch had been decorated with coloured lights and the traditional holly wreath was hanging from the front door. We had hung up a stocking for our baby daughter, put some extra logs on the already roaring fire and were just drawing the curtains for the night, when I looked out of the window and saw a battery of twinkling lights coming up the driveway. It was the lanterns of the local church choir. There were eight of them. They were all muffled up against the cold and were dragging a tiny oilskin-protected organ behind them.

They were not entirely unexpected, for Sinclair had warned us that we could expect a visit from the village choir, so we had already prepared a large bowl of mulled ale and plenty of mince pies.

We couldn't leave them out there in the falling snow, picturesque as it did look, so we invited them all into our spacious hall.

The organ was hauled up the steps by many willing hands, their wellingtons and wet jackets were deposited in the porch, and we started to make inroads on the mulled ale.

Once everyone was warm and in a suitably convivial mood, the organ burst into life and we had our own personal choir for more than an hour. We were happy to join in the hymn singing and complimented them on their highly professional performance.

After so much singing it was necessary to quench their thirst once again and hand out more mince pies.

Our carollers were somewhat reluctant to leave and I gathered that we would be at the top of their list for next Christmas Eve 'Wassailing'.

As their lanterns slowly receded down the driveway, we gazed out on the softly falling snow, the silent night and the majesty of stars in the heavens, and gave thanks to The Lord for our many blessings.

Brook House, as the name would suggest, had a brook running along one side of it. Right at the entrance the brook plunged into a deep ditch which would sometimes overflow into the road in the winter. As the entrance was also at the convergence of two steep hills, it could sometimes result in a fast flowing stream 3ft deep.

One night I was just settling down in front of a nice fire with a good book, when the phone rang.

It was a cry for help! Apparently five of the local farmers' wives had been to a meeting of the Women's Institute and were stranded on the far side of the stream. Could I bring a wheelbarrow down and ferry them across?

I put on my raincoat and wellingtons, placed an electric lantern in the wheelbarrow and sallied forth to investigate.

One look was enough for me to know that the wheelbarrow idea was a non-starter. When I waded into the stream the icy cold water immediately came over the top of my wellingtons, filled them and then continued up to my knees. The girls hooted with laughter and thought this was very funny.

The only thing was, I should have to carry them across. I am 6ft tall and pretty strong, but farmer's wives are well fed and not of the dainty variety. I had visions of my knees buckling, and tripping up in the flood, with a 14-stone female sitting on my head.

"Come on, Mr Orrell – take me in your arms and carry me across as if I were a baby!"

Screams of laughter...

"Some baby!"

Amidst much hilarity, I hoisted them up one by one and ferried them across without mishap, although I must admit that the 14-stoner who had wanted to be carried like a baby had a near miss.

Having deposited them safely on the other side, and been suitably embraced, I hurried back home, changed my soaking wet trousers, poured myself a large Scotch and continued with my book.

My little herd of cows gave me much pleasure and I began to wish that it were possible to expand.

I went to see the farmer whose land adjoined ours and tried to tempt him to sell me a few acres. He did tell me that he would consider it, but eventually decided that even though he would receive an inflated price, it would make his own farm an uneconomical proposition.

We dearly loved our beautiful home and the picturesque country around Huxley, but 14½ acres could never provide us with a full-time living. We really were in a turmoil as to what to do. I'd had a taste of honey as it were, and wanted more.

Every summer's day when I went over to Ellesmere Port and closed myself in my dark little consulting room, my spirit was reaching out to green fields and corn waving in the breeze.

I really would have liked to have given up optics and farmed full time. That was easier said than done.

By this time we had got two small children who would require educating.

We came up with the idea that perhaps we should sell up, buy a farm and get it running so that it would provide us with a reasonable living. In the meanwhile I should have to continue with my optics until that lucky day.

Little did I realise the enormous capital that would be involved and the many heartaches which lay ahead.

CHAPTER 11

MASSEY HOUSE FARM
(We take a gamble)

The time had come to move on. We decided that beautiful as Brook House was, it was an awful lot of work with its elegant lawns and beds of 500 roses, plus all the paths and driveways which required constant weeding.

We found that the experiment with our tiny herd of six cows had opened up wider vistas.

A 'proper farm' would be the thing.

We would be able to employ more labour and – who knows – I might eventually be able to farm full-time!

With this germ of an idea I began to read more and more books on farming.

We visited a number of farms that were for sale. Most of them had snags – they were too expensive, the houses were impossible, or we didn't like the layout.

We were quite taken with one particular farm of 60 acres. It had a pedigree Jersey Herd, and had as its boundary a lovely forest of silver birches. I decided to seek the advice of a farming patient of mine.

"If you want it as a hobby it would be fine, but it's too small as a commercial proposition and situated where it is it will probably fetch too much money," was his advice.

It was alongside Delamere Forest, not far from Manchester and in the 'Stockbroker Belt'.

My farmer friend was right. We went to the auction and the price it made was sky-high.

Eventually we espied an advert for a 120-acre farm near Whitchurch, Shropshire. The farm was in the centre of a little village called Whixall.

It was approached by a rising driveway, about 500 yards long. The house, which was T-shaped, stood at the far end of a large square cobbled yard, which had a midden in the centre.

Outside the kitchen door, which faced into the yard, there was a well – the only source of water on the farm.

We were invited into the kitchen, which was of medium size with a beamed ceiling and a large steel open range with a leaking water tap on the side.

The farmer was a tall sparse man of about 75. His spinster sister was about the same age.

They were a very solemn pair and appeared to have reached the stage where, both draped in sacking aprons, they sat one each side of the old range and dreamt of the past.

'Old Bill', as he came to be known, had a permanent dewdrop on the end of his nose. I was fascinated as to when it would eventually fall.

We were taken on an inspection of the house. In the first bedroom we came to, an ancient female in the bed hastily buried her head under the bedclothes. We came to another bedroom which was piled up with all sorts of junk. In one corner there was an enamel bath.

"You see that bath? Do you know, I've had that bath for 20 years and I've never used it!"

We were given a plan of the various fields and left on our own to walk the farm. It was split into two sections, with approximately 30 acres on the other side of a narrow lane. It was mostly down to permanent pasture, apart from 10 acres of rye.

The hedgerows were overrun with rabbits and the gates, where there were any, were dropping in pieces and held up with string. The soil appeared rich and tillable but was obviously suffering from long-term neglect. All the hedges were 15 feet high with large gaps and badly in need of laying. The ditches were overgrown and the drains were blocked and overflowing.

Back at the farmyard there was the same tale of utter neglect. The calf pens were four feet deep in litter and the shippon was filthy, with cobbled floors, rotten wooden stalls and sacks over the windows to replace broken glass.

There were also two major problems: (a) there was no electricity and (b) the only water for the whole farm, apart from the pits in the fields, was a hand-primed pump at the kitchen door. The pits from which the existing herd had been drinking were of course 'taboo' for an attested herd. What to do? Decisions! Decisions!

First of all I went to see Wyatt Bros of Whitchurch. They were a big firm who specialised in anything to do with water. Unless we could get a supply of clean unadulterated water, we would not get an attested licence.

Bill Wyatt came out to the farm, did a series of tests, and went through all the ancient surveys of the area. He came to the conclusion that we would be pretty certain to strike water if we sank a bore hole deep enough.

If we struck suitable water, the Ministry would give us a grant towards the whole project, including piping out water to all the fields. If we did not strike water, we would get nothing and would have to pay the cost of the borehole!

We could see that there were possibilities for the place and that the land when limed, fertilised and re-seeded, would come to life. But there would be a lot of hard work and money to be spent before we would reap any benefit, and of course, there was the big gamble over the water. It depended on what price the farm would make at the forthcoming auction.

The fatal day arrived. I drove over to Whitchurch with butterflies in my stomach and fingers crossed.

After the usual reading of the particulars (see Appendix i), which of course described the farm in such glowing terms that I wondered if I was at the right auction, the bidding started at what I thought was a promising figure, so I joined in. It quickly went up by £500 at a time and then started to slow down until there were just two of us in it. I had just reached the top limit to which I thought we ought to go, when the hammer fell on my last bid. What a relief! It was ours, for better or for worse, for £14,500. Within five minutes I was approached by a big ginger-haired farmer who offered me a profit of £1,000 if I would sell it to him. I was not interested in a profit, even if he had offered me £5,000.

I could not get home quickly enough to break the good news to Sheila, who of course, had been keeping the practice going in Ellesmere Port.

We had still got to sell our beautiful country estate. I had been promised a bridging loan to purchase the farm, but this of course would cost money, so it was imperative that we sell as quickly as possible. The estate agent advised putting it up for auction, so we agreed to this.

The auction was arranged to take place at the Blossoms Hotel in Chester at 2pm. At 11am on the auction day, the head of the firm arrived at Brook House. He informed us that he had received an offer of what he considered was the value of the house, but the offer would only be open until 12 noon. He strongly advised us to take it, stressing that a bird in the hand is worth two in the bush. I was in a quandary, as I knew that there were several people who appeared to be keen on the property, but of course I did not know who the mystery bidder was.

We decided to sell. At 2.30pm I got a phone call from a very angry man who had gone to the auction in Chester, only to find that it had been cancelled. He had been quite prepared to pay at least £1,500 more than our mystery buyer. We realised afterwards that we had probably been 'taken for a ride', but it is easy to be wise after the event. The mystery buyer turned out to be a complete stranger who had not even done a tour of inspection.

CHAPTER 12

THE MOVE TO MASSEY HOUSE FARM

Once all the legalities had been sorted out and the farm was officially ours, we started to plan the removal. It was not going to be easy. During our stay at Brook House we had acquired, amongst other things – a small daughter and an even smaller son, six heifers, three calves, two hunters, two cats, two Staffordshire Bull Terriers and 20 hens. Also a Ferguson tractor and trailer with various implements, a Land Rover, an Austin 10 and a 2.5 litre Jaguar. All these had to be transported to our new farm, plus of course our household furniture. One of us had to be there to meet them.

With the help of a few friends, everything arrived safely. It was early evening by the time that things were reasonably sorted. Kerry and Ventry had been put in one field and the heifers turned out to graze in another.

We had previously scoured out a small barn with disinfectant and put in six steel partitions, so that we could bring our little herd in for milking. We would not of course be able to sell TT milk until we had a proper water supply and fulfilled all the other requirements for an attested herd. Meanwhile our surplus milk would be collected along with that of our neighbours, none of whom were attested.

Our first night at Massey House Farm made us realise that we could wave goodbye to all the creature comforts to which we had become accustomed. The first thing on arriving was the need for the good old British cup of tea. The hard facts of life began to emerge. The only water supply at that time was from the antiquated hand pump outside the kitchen door, and it had to be primed by pouring a jug of water down its mouth and then pumping away energetically to get it started. It was therefore necessary to remember always to retain a small amount of water for priming. After having 'borrowed' a jug of water, it had to be heated either on the kitchen fire, or by starting up a primus stove. We had of course no electricity. Anyway, nothing daunted, we started up the primus stove, brewed our tea and then made good use of the frying pan to rustle up an enormous meal of bacon, eggs and sausages.

We sat and chatted about our new life in front of the big open fire, and when it started to get dark we lit our numerous new oil lamps and thought how romantic it was! Until we suddenly started to itch. We got out our electric torch and examined our legs closely. To our horror we found that we were alive with fleas.

'Old Bill' and his sister, who apparently hadn't had a bath for 20 years, if ever, were obviously tougher characters than we were, and must have become immune to the creatures.

We prayed that the bedroom would be flea-free and decided to strip off downstairs, then sprint upstairs hopefully before the fleas arrived.

It took a week of scrubbing and disinfecting before we could sit in the kitchen again.

We were somewhat intrigued by the numerous pieces of brown paper which were stuck on the kitchen wall. When we removed the first one, we found that it was a very practical solution for holding in the loose plaster, which started to cascade onto the floor.

The next day when our natural functions demanded attention, we discovered that there was a very matey two-seater drop-down privy about 50 yards away in the back garden -- a cheering thought for when it was a cold winter's night and pouring with rain.

Our first priority was to obtain an adequate water supply. On the original survey we had been assured that if we sank a bore hole deep enough we stood a 90 per cent chance of striking water.

The Wyatt Bros workmen eventually arrived with all their gear. Basically it consisted of a high tripod from which was suspended a heavy steel drilling rod on a wire. By means of gearing, operated by a tiny petrol engine, the rod was lifted to the top of the tripod, then released so that it hit the ground with a resounding bang and gradually drove itself deeper and deeper.

Two morose-looking men arrived each day at 8.30am and started the apparatus in motion.

As the rod dug down tubes were inserted to keep the hole open. After 10 days and reaching 90 feet I was getting extremely worried. I used to go out each morning, and say, "Any sign of water?"

"Nay, sometimes all us gets is salt water."

At 200 feet they struck salt water.

"Dost tha want us to go on?"

I didn't know what to do. If we didn't strike water I would get no Government grant and would have to pay for the whole operation,

"Yes, you better go a bit deeper," I replied

The next two days were a nightmare. Then – joy, oh joy – at 214 feet there was water spouting 15 feet into the air! What's more it was unadulterated and a seemingly endless supply.

We certainly got the whisky out that night. This was wonderful news: we would soon be able to have a bath.

The first thing we did was to get Wyatts to lay pipes out to all the fields and install drinking troughs. A plumber was then contacted and two bathrooms and a kitchen were installed in the farmhouse.

There was no possibility of mains electricity reaching the district for several years, so we installed a large and expensive Petter automatic diesel lighting plant. This was the latest and most sophisticated apparatus and should have been foolproof. When a light was switched on it was supposed to start up the plant automatically, and when the last light was switched off, the plant would switch off. We had an awful lot of trouble with the automatic gear and eventually rigged up a Heath Robinson series of pulleys and wire, terminating in a piece of string over our bed, which we used to pull to shut the beast down. This did the trick if some idiot had not left a light on in one of the remote wagon sheds. If this happened the plant would not shut down and it would necessitate one of us getting out of bed to find the offending light, or going into the engine house and closing the plant down by pulling up two levers until the beast was silent. Neither were pleasant options on a wet and cold night. Our Heath Robinson contraption was 100 per cent successful and we remained warm and cosy in bed.

Having running water and electricity made all the difference to our lives and we could now start to plan ahead.

But whoah! What about my optical practice in Ellesmere Port, 35 miles away and, before the farm got going, our only source of income? I certainly had a hard life ahead of me for the foreseeable future.

Obtaining labour did not seem to be a problem in our village. Most of the men had their own smallholdings of a few acres and were only too glad to have the chance of earning a little extra money now and then.

When we eventually struck water, it was necessary to erect a small building to house the pump and its bits and pieces. Cecil and Henry were the chosen locals to do the job. Cecil was a tall, pale and humourless individual, a pillar of the church and husband of the local schoolmistress. Henry was a good-natured young man of about 25. Cecil, being the elder of the two and the self-appointed expert, did the brickwork, and Henry did the 'navvying.' All seemed to be going well until they started to put in the floor. The hut was only about 6ft x 4ft, and when I looked in on my way to work, they had already got in about 9ins of strong cement.

"Don't you think that the floor is strong enough now, Cecil?"

"Oh no, it's not right yet!"

On the third morning when I looked in, Henry was still wheeling in barrow loads of cement, and Cecil was chucking in large stones and brick ends. By this time the floor must have been about 2ft thick.

"I think that should do now, Cecil. It's only a small pump and there won't be any vibration."

"Very well, if you say so, but it has got to be strong enough if it's going to have my name on it!"

On another memorable occasion Cecil and Henry were doing some alterations to the piggeries, and had nearly finished for the day. Henry had apparently mixed slightly more cement than they needed, so they decided that rather than waste it, they would use the surplus to fill in a gap in a wall, which was about 12ft away. The board on which the cement had been mixed was transferred on to Henry's back. He was on his hands and knees, crawling across the yard, while Cecil was quite unconcernedly turning over the cement with his trowel on this human table.

We certainly had our funny moments on the farm. All was not drudgery – I loved the open-air life and very often in the spring I would be out at 6am, start up the tractor and do two hours harrowing or rolling. I would then jump into my car and drive away to my other life of optics.

When we first went to the farm, we had not been there long before three members of the War Agricultural Committee arrived and wanted to know what I intended to do with the fields. We had not realised, as it had not been disclosed at the auction, that the farm had apparently had an order slapped on it for bad husbandry.

The tallest of the trio, who was obviously the spokesman, opened the door of his car and brought out a big wad of official-looking papers.

"Nah then, we'd like to walk the fields with you and we will make a note of what you intend doing with each field."

I was quite unprepared for this unsolicited visit and not at all happy about it. At this stage in my agricultural life I had quite a lot of theoretical knowledge, but had yet to put it into practice. These were three hard-headed, seemingly successful farmers who were about to put me through the hoop.

Ninety-five per cent of the fields were in permanent pasture and had obviously not been re-seeded for many years. I had taken a number of tests and was aware that there was a high degree of acidity in most of the fields.

"What is going to be your general policy for the farm?"

"Well, basically I intend running it as a dairy farm and selling attested milk; we will then progress on to pigs and poultry."

"Good! We had better get out and look around the fields."

After we had walked over half of the farm, they agreed that I would have an uphill fight to get it back to full production. They were appalled at all the blocked drains and overgrown hedgerows.

"What will be your first priority?"

"My first priority will be to lime most of the fields, as this will release a lot of the fertility which is at present lying dormant."

This seemed to impress them.

"Then I intend to plough, cultivate and re-seed a number of the fields."

"What sort of mixtures will you use?"

"I am a great believer in Italian Ryegrass. It is such a strong grower that I will hope to get two crops in the year. It is also one of the first grasses to sprout in the spring."

"What about your permanent pasture? Do you intend to plough up the lot?"

"No! I will certainly keep some of the old leys, but will aim to improve their productivity."

"Oh, and how will you do that?"

"Well, I shall lime them to begin with, then I shall go over them with the chain harrows and apply a fertiliser after I get a report of which minerals they are deficient in. All the thistles will be cut twice a year and the mower will be run across after each grazing in order to stimulate new growth."

"That sounds a very good start. We have seen enough, so we will leave you to get on with your work. We will visit you again in six months. I do not think that you are in need of any supervision at the moment, but if you want any advice, please give us a ring."

The three wise men returned to their car and I breathed a sigh of relief!

True to their word, they did return in six months and when they saw our bumper crops of hay and corn waving in the breeze, they were mightily impressed. They said that there was no further need for a supervision order but they would be most interested to be given the opportunity of following our future progress.

Early days on the farm were really hard graft. We had a big overdraft and large bills for all sorts of equipment such as tractors, harrows, discs, rollers, milking machines and sterilisers. We already had a Land Rover which proved to be a marvellous maid of all work, from taking the kids to school to dragging a large roller.

Before we started to produce, the strictest economies were necessary so the chief labourer was myself. My weekends and evenings were used to the full. It was not long before I had my little gang of helpers. A newcomer in any village is always a novelty and I was no exception.

At the entrance to the farm there was a smallholding occupied by the Heath family, a cheerful and numerous band of youngsters. As soon as I started ploughing, Derek, who was about 13, and one of his younger brothers, Desmond, would jump out of the bushes and land, one on each rear mudguard of my Ferguson tractor (unheard of in these days of innumerable safety regulations). They absolutely loved it, and I was glad to have their young and cheerful company. It was not long before I discovered that their one aim in life was to drive a tractor. Farm kids are naturals and after a few basic lessons I had two acting, unpaid but very enthusiastic tractor drivers. It was amazing, with a bit of organising, what we got through.

I would start ploughing on a Saturday morning at 6am. Derek and Desmond would appear about 8.30am, each with a jam 'butty' clasped in his hand. I would previously have attached my other Ferguson tractor to a set of disk harrows and my Land Rover to a set of chain harrows.

Desmond would follow me on the tractor dragging the discs and Derek would follow him in the Land Rover dragging the chain harrows.

In this fashion, with the aid of my little helpers, we would by the end of the day have a field ready for planting out with wheat.

I kept them well supplied with lemonade, cakes and some pocket money, and they loved it.

It is a pity that today's kids are spending all their spare time glued to the television or tinkering with computers. I think the risk of brain damage in later life is on a par with whatever risk they ran driving tractors.

Derek came to work for me on the farm later on when he left school.

I did the journey to Ellesmere Port five days a week, and kept the weekends free for my farming pursuits.

We started off with Clifford, a local lad, as our farm worker. It was going to be very difficult to increase our herd until we had got a new shippon, but there was plenty of work for us to do – such as double-fencing the entire farm.

I had got planning permission to build a shippon for 60 cows and had already engaged a firm to build it. The hold-up was in obtaining the steel trusses for the roof. It was just after the war and steel was still rationed.

I used my lunch hours in Ellesmere Port to scour all the steel works in Birkenhead to plead for the necessary steel. Eventually I succeeded, and work commenced.

I had decided that my new shippon should be as labour-saving as possible, so with that aim in view:

- First of all it had to have a centre passageway wide enough to drive a tractor through.
- The stalls would be arranged on each side.
- A glazed feeding trough would be in front of each cow, and they would have individual automatic drinking bowls.
- A large number of clear perspex sheets would be incorporated in the roof, so that there would be plenty of light.
- A slate would be let into the wall in front of each cow with her name on and a record of her daily rations according to her milk yield.
- The next important thing was milking arrangements. At that time there was a local firm experimenting with an overhead track system. This consisted of a railway type line suspended from the roof, running the complete length of the shippon.
- Four spring balances were attached to the line on rollers and the milk churns were then hooked on to the scales. This meant that the cows could be milked straight into the churns.
- A series of turntables ran down the central line, so that the churns could be rolled between the stalls on either side, and when full then went back onto the central line, and on to the dairy, where the milk was cooled by an in-churn cooler.

The advantage of this system was that one man could milk four cows at a time and at the end the milk was ready for off. It also had the advantage that the scales automatically recorded each cow's milk yield.

This is the system I decided to install, and even today I don't think it's been improved on.

Later on when the shippon was built and fully operational, one man used to regularly feed, use a strip cup, wash, milk and record 60 cows twice a day.

Whilst we were waiting for the shippon to be built I decided that we ought to at least try and establish the nucleus of an attested herd.

I got in touch with Reg Roberts again. He specialised in supplying in-calf Ayrshire heifers straight from Scottish attested farms. Reg guaranteed all his cattle and if there proved to be anything wrong with them he would exchange them without question. The first batch of ten arrived in the middle of the night and were there in the field to greet us next morning. We dare not bring them in to the old shippon (which we had demolished, anyway) for fear of infection. So we made one small shed safe, by going over it with a flame gun and disinfectant, and then put in standings for six. The cattle lay out, often in the snow, all that first winter, and as they calved were brought in, six at a time, to be milked. Ayrshires are renowned for their toughness and having come down from the colder climate of Scotland, they wintered very well.

By the summer the new shippon was all but finished and by the autumn we had a super herd of 60 attested heifers luxuriating in their new home.

By this time we had acquired George, our herdsman, Colin, our tractor driver, and Arthur, our general handyman. George was quite a find. He was 35 years of age, about 5ft 9ins tall, ruddy-complexioned and moved with the grace of a ballet dancer. He was a hard worker and had a long experience of working with cattle. He was a perfectionist: everything had to be exactly right.

When I arrived home at night, the first thing I did was to go into the shippon and turn on the light. Even in the middle of winter it was beautifully warm, there was a lovely aroma of sweet hay, all the cows would be munching contentedly, the whole shed was spotlessly clean and you could put a straight edge along the straw on which they were bedded.

Colin, who was slightly younger than George, was an easy-going character. Nothing seemed to worry him – he had a perpetual smile on his face and worked in a slightly lower gear than George. He became our tractor man and relief milker.

Arthur was pale-faced, older and smaller than the other two, but he seemed to have plenty of energy when things really mattered. He had all the innate cunning and skills of the old countryman and was a wizard on hedge-laying, drainage and mole-catching. He could also turn his hand to bricklaying or any other job that came along, preferably not concerning livestock unless absolutely necessary.

Mrs Teggin, who did the dairy night and morning, was a kindly plump soul of about sixty. She was a widow and lived in a small cottage in the village with her semi-invalid son. The children adored her, as did we also.

Having got our herd of cows, the next thing was to get a bull to keep them happy. But first of all we had to build a bull pen.

There was a large barn alongside the shippon that was split into various sections. We took one of these which was about 12ft square and built a feeding trough in one corner, with a massive catching yoke above, so that we could control the bull for foot trimming, etc. The front of the pen was left open and fitted with a large steel door, which he could just look over to inspect his harem as they trooped in and out on their way for milking.

Now that we had got a bull pen, the next step was to get a suitable bull to put in it.

One of the leading lights in the Ayrshire field was a Cheshire farmer named Ken Smith, who ran a prize-winning herd at The Mile House Farm near Crewe, Cheshire. I went to see Ken and was greatly impressed by the superb quality of his stock. We immediately gelled and formed the basis of a lifelong friendship.

All Ken's stock at that time were making prices in the thousands, so he suggested that I had a young pedigree bull calf, which would be considerably cheaper, and meanwhile use artificial insemination until he matured.

When we got him home and put him in our new bull pen, it was hard to visualise that some day it would be necessary to catch him in the massive yoke for treatment.

A mature Ayrshire bull can be a highly dangerous creature to have around, so I did not feel that it was worth taking any silly chances. Derek, one of my farming neighbours, used to let his bull run out with the milking herd and then chain him up with the cows when they came in for milking. He reckoned to have made quite a pet of him. Unfortunately, one day, something must have upset this bull and he attacked Derek and tossed him, inflicting injuries to his back from which he never fully recovered.

Ken Smith also ran a renowned herd of pedigree Large White pigs, so a bit later on we decided to buy a young boar and four young gilts, and thereby enter the field of pig breeding.

Initially they were allowed the run of a small field at the front of the house. All was quiet for a few months, until one night we were kept awake by squeals and grunts of satisfaction. We knew that our young boar had suddenly become aware of the facts of life and was distributing his favours amongst his harem.

In anticipation of a big increase in the pig population, we bought four large pig arks. These were put in another field and when we felt that the gilts were about to farrow they were transferred into the arks, which were specially fitted with guard rails so that the weaners had a place of safety to retreat to after they had finished suckling.

Many was the freezing cold night spent with a hurricane lamp in one of the arks waiting for the farrowing to take place. The thing to do was to break the umbilical cord as the piglets arrived, dry them and place them behind the crush barrier until they became steady on their feet. Left to herself, the mother could very well have lain on and crushed all her litter.

That reminds me of one particular night in the middle of winter. It had been snowing and I had had a particularly bad drive home from my practice in Ellesmere Port. The entrance driveway to the farm was covered with a foot of snow. I took my usual fast run at it and arrived in the farmyard to find that the whole of the place was in darkness. Oh no! The confounded Petter lighting plant had broken down again. I grabbed my torch, struggled out of the car and opened the kitchen door. On the table were two flickering candles. I became aware of a faint squealing, which seemed to be coming from the bathroom. I opened the door, and to my amazement was greeted by seven little piglets running around the floor, obviously delighted with the warmth issuing from the large hot water cylinder.

Our third child, Jane, had only been born a few weeks previously and Sheila had obviously retreated to the bedroom. I went upstairs.

"Sorry to give you a fright dear, but one of the sows in the arks farrowed a couple of hours ago and because of the cold I was afraid that the piglets would get overlain and crushed, so I brought them into the bathroom until they livened up," she explained.

"Great, but they will have to go back to their mum to be fed!" I added.

There was no shirking. They had to go back as soon as possible, otherwise they would miss the colostrum – the first milk which prevents them from scouring. I put them all carefully into a large cardboard box, covered the top with a towel, lit a hurricane lamp and struggled out into the snow. When I opened the ark door and went inside, Mum was obviously very relieved to see me. She lay down and offered her capacious udder to her starving family, who snuggled up with squeals of delight. Once I was assured that things were going according to plan, I closed the door of the ark, hurried back to the house and went straight up to bed to thaw out my frozen limbs.

Now that our pig-breeding project was well underway and we were getting litters of eight to ten little piglets, we found that there was an urgent necessity to provide the youngsters with suitable and warm accommodation once they had been weaned. We had inherited a row of broken down old-fashioned outdoor pigsties, where the poor creatures would have no option but to lie in their own excrement.

Arthur was a wizard at improvisation and soon set to work to improve things. First of all we knocked out the filthy old brick floors and then put down a six-inch layer of compacted straw for insulation. This was then covered in six inches of concrete. Contrary to general belief, pigs are intelligent and clean creatures, given the chance, so we provided them with a dung passage. This served the double purpose of allowing the pigs to keep themselves clean and of making it easier to muck out. We then raised the asbestos roof and put nine-inch straw pallets underneath for insulation. We also fitted proper glazed feeding troughs and automatic water bowls.

An amusing little incident occurred one day, relating to the pigs. It was a bright summer's day and in the afternoon I found that my last two appointments in my optical practice had been cancelled, so I decided to go home early. I arrived in the farmyard and was putting my car into the garage, when I saw two little pigs scampering across the yard and just about to go out through the gate. Somehow they must have escaped from the piggery. I ran across to investigate. Just outside the yard there was our large midden. Each day after milking, George used to sweep out the shippon and barrow the muck over to the midden. In the summer it was of a very liquid nature. Our two little pigs had contrived to get themselves in the middle of this morass and were slowly sinking. I was in a dilemma as to what to do. If I had been in my working clothes I would have waded in and grabbed them, but having just returned from my practice, I was dressed in a decent suit. What was I to do? Was I to let the pigs drown in a sea of muck or ruin my suit? If I had gone to change, they would have disappeared by the time I returned.

Fortunately, just in the nick of time, George came running down the field. He had finished milking, turned the cows out and was on his way back. He had got his wellingtons on, of course, so it was no problem. He just grabbed them by their ears and hauled them out.

I often wonder what decision I would have taken if George had not come to the rescue. My suit was worth considerably more than the piglets, BUT...?

When we took over the farm, the only standing crop was a five-acre field of rye, which at that time was an unusual crop to grow. When we came to harvest it we realised why it wasn't popular.

This was in the days before combine harvesters and so it was cut with a machine called a binder that used to bind the corn into sheaves and throw them out. The nature of the sheaves was that they were so prickly they would cut your hands to shreds. The good part was that the rye threshed out well and at a much higher price than oats or wheat.

As a result of our visit from the War Agricultural Committee we were required to grow 20 acres of wheat, five acres of oats and an acre of potatoes.

The potatoes caused the most trouble. They are a specialised crop and if you are going to grow them in any quantity you need special machinery. My tractor man had to have tuition from the agricultural sales rep who was trying to sell us a potato planter. He got the ridges done all right but when it came to splitting the ridges and dropping the seed potatoes in, things went horribly wrong. He proceeded along the first row, not looking back, with showers of potatoes hurling six feet into the air. The rest of the staff, who of course had come to see how this new-fangled machine worked, were doubled up with laughter and didn't let him forget it in a hurry.

The winters in those early days in Shropshire were tough. Central heating was only to be found in schools, hospitals and other public buildings.

Many were the mornings when we scraped the ice off our bedroom window. We had to rely on good old open fires for our heat.

The dairy was a different matter. We needed many gallons of hot water night and morning to wash the milking machines and buckets, etc. We also needed hot water for mixing the calves' meal and pig meal.

We decided to fit a large coke-fired boiler in the cellar and let it feed a huge hot-water cylinder in the bathroom. This apparatus produced vast quantities of hot water but the snag was, that for some reason the plumber hadn't fitted any control valves and when there was a high wind it was uncontrollable. In the middle of the night you would hear a rumbling like thunder – it was the hot-water cylinder jumping up and down, and one of us would have to get up and drain off the surplus until it settled down. One night there was a tremendous bang when the boiler blew up and flooded the cellar. Fortunately by that time we were at last on mains electricity and were able to replace it with a thermostatically-controlled electric cistern.

Our herd of cows was programmed to calve down in the winter months, as that was the time when milk was at its dearest. This was all well and good if the calving took place during the day when George would deal with it, but there were many times when we were awakened at 3am by all the cows in the shippon starting to roar and bellow. We knew that one of the cows had become unchained and was wandering about, or else a calving was about to take place. So there was nothing for it but for me to stagger out of bed, drag on an old coat which I kept by the side of the bed, and hurry across to the shippon. At least it was nice and warm once I got inside.

Sometimes the newly-born calf would have dropped just behind the cow and would be lying there, but doing its best to get onto its tiny feet. At other times the nose and front feet would be sticking out of the cow's posterior and she would be moaning and straining in her attempts to expel it. Unless I was prepared to stay

Sheila - "my blue-eyed blonde".   Jack on honeymoon in Wales.

A poignant portrait taken on Jack's embarkation leave.

Staff Sgt Orrell in the Middle East.   *Baby Anne at Brook House.*

Sheila and Anne by the wendy house in the garden of Brook House, close to a lake with an island in the centre.

IT'S MUCK YOU WANT!

Anne (above left) and Richard (above right) pictured on outings to the seaside when they were small children.

Sheila and Jane in the garden at Massey House Farm.

IT'S MUCK YOU WANT!

Massey House Farm, Whixhall, Shropshire as it was in 1951 when the Orrells bought the property. It is 'T'-shaped.

The back section of Massey House Farm, facing the farmyard.

IT'S MUCK YOU WANT!

George, Colin and Arthur.

Mrs Teggin, who did the dairy night and morning, pictured with Lad the Staffordshire Bull Terrier and two of the farm cats.

Arthur, collecting eggs.

IT'S MUCK YOU WANT!

Above: part of the farmyard showing the bull pen and the exterior of the shippon which Jack had designed to be labour-saving and ultra-modern. The concreting of the yard had been worked out by Arthur.

Above: the interior of the shippon, pictured from the centre, showing the light and airy conditions and the overhead rail track system.

IT'S MUCK YOU WANT!

Left: Fred, the Ayrshire bull

*Below left: a newborn calf and its mother.
Below right and bottom: some of Fred's progeny – a few of the beautiful heifers in the attested herd.*

IT'S MUCK YOU WANT!

Left: Skeleton of the experimental poultry unit.

Right: exterior of the completed experimental poultry unit.

Below: Richard and Jane in the new poultry unit.

IT'S MUCK YOU WANT!

Left: Richard and Anne helping their father with the chickens.

The Orrells on holiday with friends at Llangranog.

IT'S MUCK YOU WANT!

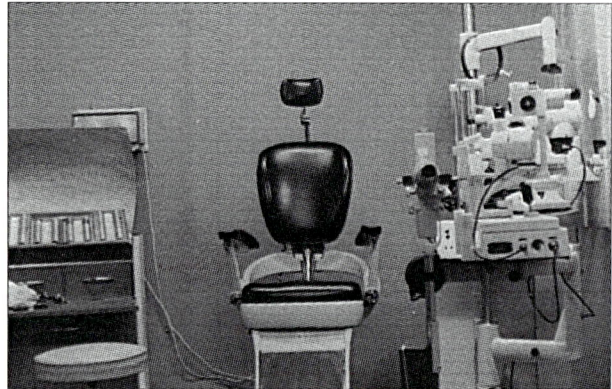

Left: Jack's consulting room in his practice at Ellesmere Port. He had a second practice in Gt Sutton. He retired when he was 66 years old.

Right: Muriel's friendly smile at reception.

Optician Bill Wilson also worked for Jack and commuted between the two practices.

Sheila filled in for occasional absences.

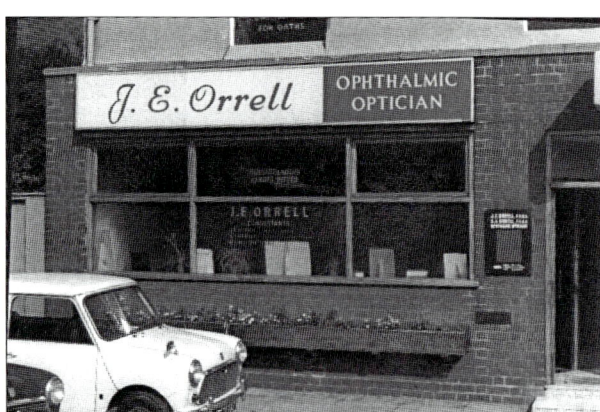

Left: Outside the Ellesmere Port practice.

A third practice at New Brighton had been purchased by the time Jack's son Richard qualified as an optician and was made a partner.

IT'S MUCK YOU WANT!

A few of the 60 cars that Jack owned which are mentioned in the book

Right: The Ford Zodiac - fast, comfortable but hard to drive on icy roads.

Left: 3.4 Jaguar and the Welton 14 caravan at Bala Lake.

Right: The elegant Allard - it had a 3ltr Ford V8 engine and attracted groups of admirers wherever it was parked! Sadly, it proved to be unreliable.

Left: Mark VII Jaguar towing the GP 14 dinghy.

IT'S MUCK YOU WANT!

Left: MGB GT.

Right: Ford Granada 3ltr coupé.

Left: The 280SL Mercedes Coupé outside the practice.

Right: E-type Jaguar.

IT'S MUCK YOU WANT!

A few of the 17 boats that Jack owned

'Tamba' GP 14, the first of many custom-built boats.

'Golden Eagle', one of two Liverpool Bay Falcons.

Left: 'Water Music' Flying Dutchman.

Right: 'Magic Dragon', a Moody 33ft twin keel, with a striking rainbow-coloured sail, racing in Scotland.

IT'S MUCK YOU WANT!

Right: 'Magic Dragon' Moody 33.

Left: 'Coquette' Contessa 32.

Right: 'Jansfin' Fin Sailer 37.

Above: 'Fiddler of Orwell' Hustler 35, with Richard, Ann and the three grandchildren.

Above: Sheila, the intrepid crew, pictured during one of the couple's sailing holidays.

Jack, aged 70, helming at sea in 1985. He finally gave up sailing in his mid-eighties – after two hip replacement operations.

Left: 'Caldy Wood' the house at West Kirby where the Orrells lived after they sold Massey House Farm.

Right: 'Caldy Wood' was situated on top of a hill and had natural sandstone rockeries all around it.

The Orrells' one-acre garden on the banks of Menai Straits has four ponds and hundreds of heathers and azaleas. There was no garden when they moved in 22 years ago and the area pictured above was high in weeds. Jack set fire to them, reseeded the lawn – and dug out the pond when he was 80. The stone came from a local quarry.

there for possibly a couple of hours, she would need some help. The help consisted of tying a piece of rope to the protruding feet and heaving as hard as you could. She would ultimately give one great strain and 'hey presto' you would be struggling with a slippery armful of new life. It was always a thrilling moment.

The next part of the act was to carry the calf to the 'boozie' or feeding trough and cover it in salt. This would encourage the cow to lick it vigorously until it was dry. Once it was standing up, it would be introduced to the milk bar. As in the case of pigs, the foremilk or colostrum is vitally important to prevent scour, a disease to which young calves are prone and from which they frequently die.

Finally I had to gather half a hundredweight of struggling calf in my arms, stumble across an ice-covered yard and drop it on a bed of straw in the calf pen, where it had the other calves to snuggle up to.

All done, I would give the cow a big bowl of warm mash, turn off the light and crawl back to bed until 6am, when I would have to arise, wash and dress, breakfast and prepare myself for a very different sort of day, examining the eyes of the nation.

It was hard going organising and working in a very busy optical practice, where I was booked up with consultations from 9.30am until 6pm, plus doing a 70-mile journey each day, and at the same time rebuilding a more or less derelict farm – quite apart from keeping the Agricultural Mortgage Corporation and my bank manager sweet.

Ted Pollard, my bank manager in Ellesmere Port who became a close friend, had two sons who were studying at Ellesmere College, which was nearby. He used to pay us frequent visits, ostensibly to visit his sons, but I am sure he used to count the cows etc. to compare with our overdraft. Nevertheless we had many enjoyable Sundays hosting Ted and his sons.

During the years I had several secretaries in my optical practice. The outstanding one was Jean Roberts. Jean came to me as a bright star after several disastrous failures. She was young and pretty, and had a doting husband who used to arrive each day at lunchtime to collect her and take her to lunch. Jean was the perfect secretary. She made herself responsible for the rest of the staff, and carried out all the bookkeeping and incidental running of the practice meticulously. After several years, her husband David, who had a post with the Shell Refinery, was posted overseas and of course Jean had to accompany him. I was devastated and knew it would be a hard job indeed to replace her. After an absence of eight years, David was repatriated, Jean returned with him and stayed as my secretary until I retired.

My next secretary, Mrs Helen Jones, was a completely different character. She was a Scottish widow of some sixty summers. She was tall and spare, with an aquiline nose and grey hair made up into a bun. She had a refined Edinburgh accent and personality.

In her day she was reputed to have had one of the first motors and to have had a pilot's licence. She had a very large and very old Labrador named Craig which she used to bring with her each day and bed down in one corner of her office.

Mrs Jones had all the thriftiness of her race and never believed in wasting anything. All her bookkeeping was seemingly done on the backs of old envelopes, so I did not have to spend much money on stationery. No lights were permitted to be switched on during the daylight hours and any stamps which had not been franked were carefully put away in a tin box for re-use.

When she went on holiday to Scotland I used to receive colourful postcards of the scenery and details of her daily excursions, but always at the bottom, there would be a note:

"PS: Please save this for me."

She was highly efficient and reliable, and I'm sure saved me pounds.

It was my practice on a Friday to work from 9.30am to 9pm. This was to save me going in on a Saturday, thus leaving me free to carry on my farming pursuits. Sheila used to make me a small packet of sandwiches to take with me, so that if I got a break in between my appointments during the afternoon, I could grab a sandwich for sustenance. There were invariably several sandwiches left which I had not had the time to consume. Mrs Jones would regard these with a covetous eye.

"Would you no' be wanting those sandwiches, Mr Orrell?"

"No, Mrs Jones, you are very welcome to them."

"Thank ye very much, Mr Orrell. I won't eat them now, I will save them until I get home and have a hot bath. It will save me putting on the electric fire before I get to bed."

Mrs Jones was in her element if it was snowing. In addition to her other accomplishments, she had apparently been an expert skier in her youth. One year it snowed for several days, so she used to come to work on her skis. This activity was reported in the local and national press! There came a night when the snow was melting and there was only slush on the ground. When it came time to go home, undeterred, she solemnly strapped on her skis and padded off down the road, a stick in each hand. The funniest feature was that in her right hand she was also clutching a large string bag full of oranges – marmalade oranges, I believe.

CHAPTER 13

MOTORS

During the 10 years that we were on the farm, I seemed to get through an amazing number and variety of cars. Sheila once counted up to 60.

When we first went there we had a Land Rover, an old Austin 10 and a 2½ litre Jaguar – one of the old ones with enormous P100 headlamps.

The Land Rover and the Austin were kept on the farm for general use, and I started using the Jag.

I soon found out that on a daily run of about 70 miles, it was proving an expensive luxury and in view of our cash commitments it had to go. It was replaced by a Triumph Herald.

There then followed over the years a long procession of cars, the size and desirability of which fluctuated according to how well my optical practice was doing. But they did range from Austin 7s to an Oldsmobile, an NSU RO 80, an Allard, a BMW and a string of Jaguars.

One of the small cars much coveted in those early days was the Morris 1000. They were well ahead of their time and handled beautifully. They were like gold dust and had a waiting list of two years.

It so happened that at that time there was a particularly persistent cattle meal salesman who was trying to get me to give him a large monthly order.

One day Cyril arrived in a brand new grey Morris Convertible with a red hood.

"Where did you get that from, Cyril?"

"Ah, that would be telling. It's been on order a long time."

"Do you want to sell it?"

"You must be joking, it's a smashing car and I've only just got it."

"You really do want a monthly order for cattle and pig meal don't you?"

"I sure do – it would give me a big boost with the firm."

"Right! You can have it on one condition – you sell me your car."

"Oh hell! You are a hard bugger – what am I going to do my rounds in?"

"Well, you can have the use of my wife's Austin until you get a suitable replacement. Think about it."

Cyril thought about it for ten minutes and then to my great delight, handed me the keys to the Morris.

One of the cars that Sheila had was a very early open model Austin 7. It was painted dark blue and had been re-upholstered in pink leather. It had obviously had a very chequered life and at some time the seat had been replaced by a cushion, which was supported by four thin wooden planks.

On certain types of road they would set up a vibration which made it feel as if someone was beating your bottom.

In Ellesmere Port there was a firm which used to hire out taxis, and also sell the odd second-hand car. One day Ernest, my chemist friend, and I were strolling past on our way to lunch at The Station Hotel, when on Charlie Crump's Taxi Rank we espied a lovely old taxi for sale for £200.

Charlie Crump, the proprietor, was a patient of mine, so I went into his office and made enquiries.

"Yes! It's surplus to our requirements, has been serviced and is in good usable condition."

It was an enormous great Austin 18. Built like a battleship, with long running boards with the spare wheel strapped on one side and doors six inches thick. Inside it had a wind-down partition between the driver and passengers with speaking tube inter-communication. It also had two additional let-down seats so it could take five passengers in the back.

Would it be a suitable vehicle for my wife to replace the bottom-smacking Austin 7?

Well, it was so big that she would be able to wheel the baby's pram inside the back. It was a bargain too good to miss. Would they be interested in a part exchange? Yes, they would! With trepidation I drove it home that night.

"Oh, darling, I've got you a new car – do you want to come and look at it?"

When she saw it she nearly had a fit.

"It's enormous! I can't drive that thing."

"Just think of how safe it will be for the children and how much room there is – you'll be able to push the pram straight inside it."

Our two elder children of course absolutely loved it. They could wind the partition up and down, and have great fun communicating with each other through the speaking tube.

Once Sheila had calmed down and driven it she became quite fond of it.

It caused quite a lot of amusement when she drove it into Whitchurch. People naturally thought it was a taxi and tried to flag it down. After they had been picked up, they couldn't understand why they hadn't got to pay a fare.

We ran it with great success for quite a while, until it developed a fault with the self-starter, which used to jam. The only way of releasing it was to lie on your back underneath it and rotate the shaft with a large spanner. After Sheila had done this several times in the pouring rain it had to go.

And what happened to her 'Pink Panther' Austin 7? Charlie

Crump was apparently using it as a novelty vehicle in his taxi business, as one day when we walked down for our lunch, we saw it with the hood down, speeding through the town with a cargo of Chinamen, their pigtails hanging over the side. We were greatly amused. They had probably been collected off one of the ships and were being taken on a sightseeing tour of the town.

With the demise of the big Austin, Sheila had to have a replacement vehicle. I decided somewhat reluctantly to hand over my Morris 1000. She was absolutely delighted.

The loss of this super little car was somewhat placated by the acquisition of a black Allard with a 3 litre Ford V8 engine. On my way in to work each day I had espied this magnificent brute in a used car lot. An Allard had won the Monte Carlo Rally and I couldn't wait to get my hands on it.

It had what I considered a very low price on it, so I stopped and gawped. Rex Sutton the dealer ambled over. I sat inside, started the engine and revved it up. Clouds of smoke issued forth.

"How many miles has it done?"

"I don't know, the speedometer says 70,000 but it could be more. It probably wants new piston rings."

"Oh, I think that would be a waste of time – it would be as bad as ever after 5,000 miles. What it needs is a replacement engine."

"If you say so. I could do you one at cost if you're interested."

A deal was struck, and I took delivery of the car complete with new engine, in four days' time.

The Allard was a very distinctive looking car, with its long lean lines and whenever I used to park it, I would on my return find an admiring audience in attendance.

My daily run became almost enjoyable. I ran it for about 18 months and then it started to give trouble. For some reason it didn't have any waterproof protection plates underneath, and if you hit a patch of water at speed the engine would cut out and it would be a case of limping home on four cylinders. It then went through a patch of misfiring. My garage played around with it for days – they changed the plugs, leads, distributor, etc., but couldn't seem to really make it reliable.

The possibility of being stranded on my way to work and having to cancel all my appointments loomed in front of me. It was absolutely essential for me to have a foolproof car.

I got in touch with Rex Sutton again, to see what he could suggest. He rang me to say that he'd just got a Ford Zodiac that had only done 5,000 miles. I went to see it. It was in two-tone blue and looked brand new. He took back the Allard in part exchange. So we regretfully had to part. If I had had more time to find the fault I would probably have kept it for a bit longer.

The Zodiac proved to be thoroughly reliable and never let me down. It was quite fast and very comfortable. It was perfect if there was no frost about, but was light on the back and rear-wheel drive. It was a perfect pig when the roads were covered in ice, as they frequently were in Shropshire during the winter. The only thing to do then was to weigh down the back with a couple of bags of sand, but even then it very often used to proceed like a crab, with its front wheels in the middle of the road and its rear wheels in the gutter.

In later years I had similar trouble with a 280SL Mercedes Coupé – a beautiful classic, but when it was icy it wouldn't even back out of the driveway.

I have had many other cars over the years, probably the most memorable being my long string of 12 Jaguars including a superb E-type in Ferrari Maroon with a white hood.

CHAPTER 14

RATS

After we had got our lovely new shippon fully operational, and cleaned and disinfected the rest of the farm buildings, we set to work to get rid of the RATS. When we first arrived on the farm, the whole place was alive with rats as large as small cats. If you crossed the yard at night they would run across your feet. Sheila and the children were absolutely terrified of them and I can't say that I was over-keen myself.

Due to their advanced years, our predecessors had obviously long ago given up all forms of husbandry, so the rats had just taken over.

They were in the hay bays, in the piggery, in the granary – tearing up sacks of meal – and on one memorable occasion they even got into the house.

One night when I was peacefully seated at my desk, filling in the milk record sheets, I heard the most awful scream coming from above. I rushed upstairs and there was Sheila having hysterics.

She had been putting Anne, one of our daughters, to bed, had drawn back the sheet and a large rat had jumped out. I pulled Sheila and Anne out of the bedroom and quickly closed the door. I went downstairs grabbed Lassie, our Staffordshire Bull Terrier from where she had been dozing by the fire, took her upstairs, opened the bedroom door and pushed her inside.

During the next few minutes there was the most unholy din of squeals and snarls, as they engaged in their fight to the death. After a while everything went quiet, so I opened the door. There was Lassie, blood all over her muzzle, clutching a large dead rat between her paws. Needless to say she had an extra portion of meat for her supper that night.

We had already tried setting traps and poison, with very limited success, so we decided to get in touch with a pest eradication firm.

We had to enter into a long-term contract with them and eventually one of their operators arrived, clad in special overalls, gloves and goggles. He proceeded to mix up two large buckets of what was bread and rat poison which he distributed to various parts of the farmyard.

Relieved, I said to Sheila: "Well, dear, we should be all right now – these experts will soon get rid of all the rats."

Or would they!

Nothing happened: we were still having sacks of meal torn apart. Our rats appeared to be a hardened breed and to relish the bait, which they polished off at a great rate.

After four lots of treatment and no perceivable effect, we decided to try and cancel the contract, telling the firm not to carry out any more visits.

We were told that the contract had another year to run and could not be cancelled. However, I told my bank to cancel any further payments.

I was in the granary one day mixing meal, when I saw a car arrive in the yard and disgorge a large red-faced officious looking man, who was wearing a bowler hat. He knocked on the door. When Sheila opened it I heard him say in a loud voice: "Does John Edward Orrell live here? I am the County Court Bailiff and I have come to issue him with a summons for non-payment of debt."

I was surely not going to present myself to collect the summons and beat a hasty retreat to the other side of the barn.

When he had gone without issuing the summons Sheila came over to the barn doubled up with laughter.

"I have just had the County Court Bailiff here after you. What have you been up to?"

The matter was eventually resolved when I got my solicitor to write to the firm involved, pointing out that they were in breach of their contract, as they had not eradicated the rats from the premises.

Arthur, my handyman, finally came to the rescue.

"My cat's just had a litter of six kittens. What you want is six cats loose outside on the farm – they'll soon sort out the rats."

Arthur was right! We took delivery of the six kittens as soon as they were weaned. It was amazing – they eventually took complete charge of the rat problem. They each had their patch, one in the shippon, one in the piggery, and the others in the hay bay and granary. One would sit on a bag of corn, seemingly half asleep, for hour after hour but as soon as a rat appeared, it did not have a chance.

These cats were not domesticated and never came into the house. They were given large bowls of milk by George, the cowman, twice a day, and for the rest they ate cattlecake, rats and occasionally mice, and rabbits. We had no more trouble with pests.

In the early days of our arrival on the farming scene, harvesting was quite primitive. It was some time before we had sufficient funds to buy the necessary machinery and in any case we did not have much to harvest that first year.

Colin had a smallholding of five acres. He also had a magnificent 18hh Shire horse, on which he doted. For our first harvest we used a combination of Colin's horse-drawn cutter and rake, and our Ferguson tractor and trailer. The hay was cut and lay in swathes which had to be constantly turned by hand to get them to dry out. The swathes were then raked into heaps, and with the aid of pikel or pitch fork, tossed up onto the trailer.

Loading a trailer with hay is quite a skilled job. One man stays on the trailer and loads, whilst the others hurl pitch forks of hay to him from each side. It is essential to get the corners right, or the whole load can topple over. It would be regarded as a terrible disgrace if the load were to drop off on the way home, and the loader would have his leg pulled for years to come.

Anne and Richard, our two small children, absolutely loved this type of haymaking and with their beguiling smiles, would bribe the men to perch them on the swaying carts for the ride back home.

They never forgave me when I bought a Massey Harris Pick-up Baler.

The advent of the pick-up baler did of course considerably speed up harvesting. This was a wonderful invention – it had its own engine and was attached to the tractor by a power lift. You dragged it over the swathes and it proceeded to pick up the hay, and pack it solidly into a square coffin-like steel chamber. It would then bind up the baled hay with twine and drop off the 3ft long bales.

The bales were then stooked up, four or five together, and left to dry for a few days before being transported to the farm and stacked in the Dutch barn. Later on, when our new leys were producing, we often used to get two crops and we regularly used to fill our seven-bay Dutch barn up to the roof, and also have surplus stacks out in the fields which we used to sell off to some of the smallholders in the district.

To relieve the laborious job of turning the hay by hand, we also acquired a mechanical hay turner. This operated off the tractor power take-off, and in inclement weather was a great help in getting the hay dry and in condition for baling.

There is an amusing tale about the baler. It was in the middle of the hay harvest and the baler had been working flat out. It so happened that I was not at home on this particular day. Our tractor driver arrived at the kitchen door in a distraught and breathless condition, having run all the way from one of the hayfields on the other side of the road. Sheila opened the door.

"Yes, Colin, what on earth is the matter?"

"Can you ring up Burgesses quick, the 'orses 'ead's down in the bottom!"

Sheila nearly had a fit, thinking that some terrible accident had happened. When Colin calmed down, all was revealed. It appeared that the 'horse's head' was the name given to that part of the baler which goes up and down, compressing the loose hay in the form of bales in the chamber. It was in fact a heavily weighted plunger which would crash down every few seconds. This plunger had apparently worked its bolts loose and was now lying in the bottom of the chamber. Burgesses were the local agricultural agents from whom we had bought the baler. In harvest time they ran a service van full of the parts which, through experience, they thought were likely to be required. All was soon well.

Weather was the problem in harvest time. One year, once we had cut the hay and got it ready for baling, the skies would open and soak it again. When we did finally get it baled, it was of poor quality and a lot of the bales turned mouldy.

I was absolutely distracted, as by that time we had over 100 head of cattle on the farm, and hay was their basic fodder for the winter months. I would go around the fields sniffing inside the bales to see how many we could salvage.

I didn't notice it at first, but I suddenly started to wheeze and cough. I thought it was some form of hay fever, and simply took a few aspirins and bought a bottle of Campbell's Cherry Cough Cure.

After three weeks with no improvement, I decided to consult the doctor. I told him my symptoms and what I had been taking. "Ah!" he said, "I had a rep in the other day who was telling me about some new-fangled spray."

He emptied his waste-paper basket on the floor, rummaged

around in the litter, and pulled out a pamphlet.

"Here we are, I'll prescribe one of these for you, it should be just the thing for your trouble."

It turned out to be an ingenious spray which had a capsule inside it. When you put it in your mouth and inhaled, the capsule would explode and shower your lungs with a healing powder. I persevered with this wonder gadget for a fortnight, with no noticeable improvement in my condition.

We thought a holiday might be a good idea, so we drove down to Newquay in Cardigan, West Wales and hired a lovely little cottage just above the bay. Some friends who had joined us had a little sailing boat and used to invite us out for a sail. After the sail it was necessary to lift the boat onto its launching trolley and drag it across the soft sand to its parking bay.

One day it was as much as I could do to help them across the sand, I was coughing and gasping for breath.

That night I had a temperature of 104°F and felt really ill. Sheila became very worried.

"You can't go on like this, I'm going to ring for a doctor."

When the doctor arrived he said I was seriously ill, and he wanted a specialist to examine me.

The next morning a specialist arrived. After the usual tests, he looked at me and said: "You're a lucky man." (I sure didn't feel very lucky…) "You have got Farmer's Lung and it so happens that I am doing a research paper on it at the moment."

An ambulance arrived within the hour and took me to Aberystwith Hospital. It transpired that Farmer's Lung was a disease caused by inhaling the spores of musty hay.

I was regarded as an interesting specimen and given a private room and VIP treatment.

I was apparently in a pretty bad way and if I'd not received the necessary specialised treatment I would probably have died.

Poor Sheila had to pack up everything, including our three children and all their gear, and wind her way back to Shropshire.

Fortunately she was able to substitute for me in the practice at Ellesmere Port.

I was off work for eight weeks, so she had a really tough time – as she had all the travelling to do and had also to keep a watchful eye on the farm.

After this awful year with mouldy hay and torrential rain, I thought that the time had come to try silage, which at that time was a very popular substitute for hay.

We started off by digging an enormous pit and then concreted the base so as to make a solid foundation.

The procedure with silage was to cut the grass when it was very young, spread it in the pit and then compress it by driving the tractor over it. The grass was then allowed to grow again and the process repeated until the pit was full. In between each layer it was necessary to water in a mixture of molasses. When the pit was full it was covered with a sheet and left to ferment.

Well-made silage has an attractive sweet scent and the cows love it. Poorly-made silage smells awful. When it comes to feeding, it has to be cut with a silage knife, a bit like cutting peat, and can be very hard work. The only trouble is it has an all-pervading smell and even the well-made variety is noticeable a quarter of a mile away.

George, my cowman, did not like it. He, of course, was in close contact with it, and every night when he went home his wife used to make him strip completely and leave all his clothes outside! What a pity! George was a very good cowman and I didn't want to lose him. The other men's wives were also complaining of the smell.

The next year we had to go back to the vagaries of hay. We also tried a few acres of kale. If the weather was reasonable during the winter, we used to turn the cows out for a couple of hours and let them graze the kale. Their intake was controlled by an electric fence which we had to move every day.

CHAPTER 15

THE YARD

Now that we had got the dairy unit up and running, our next big project was to concrete the farmyard. This was a great big square with the farm buildings on three sides and on the fourth was the house. This was fronted by a raised grass-covered area with a small sycamore tree at one side. Vehicles calling at the house would drive round this 'island'.

Like all old-time farmyards, it had been made of cobblestones and when we first arrived there was a great heap of steaming manure in the middle, studded with the occasional broken bedstead and pieces of old farm implements. We decided right away that this would have to go. We had even toyed with the idea of having a rose bed in the middle, round which the farm traffic could turn, but realised that the island in front of the house served this purpose.

To begin with, we built a solid concrete floor just outside the farmyard and transferred all the muck to its new home.

Arthur, our handyman, was put in charge of the yard project. I had considered getting a building firm to do the job but all the estimates were way above my schedule and, of course, if we did it ourselves, the cost would be spread more gradually. The first thing that we did was to buy a new petrol-driven concrete mixer and have 20 tons of sand and 10 tons of gravel delivered. We felt that this would keep us going for quite a while. Next we had three tons of cement delivered, which we stored in the barn.

Arthur cut himself a barrow load of various length stakes which he proceeded to hammer in between the cobbles at different levels; pieces of string were then stretched between the stakes to mark out sections which he considered could be completed each day. After the cows had been milked, calves and pigs fed, and all the routine jobs done, the whole of the staff, including me, was put on concrete-mixing.

It proved to be a mighty project as we felt that to stand the weight of heavy farm machinery, milk lorries and meal deliveries, the concrete had to be at least 9ins thick. A barrow load didn't seem to make much difference. However, we pressed on under Arthur's supervision, tipping our loads of concrete into his various partitions. The job took about a month to complete, and when finished, looked superb. The whole place seemed to take on a more cheerful and efficient countenance.

Our 'Master Builder' had worked it out in his head that the whole of that huge yard would drain to one large grid – and it did! Even after the heaviest rain, there was never a puddle in the yard. Not a bad achievement for a man who had never been to school, or only very occasionally.

Apparently Arthur's father had been a real brute and many was the night that Arthur was too scared to go home, so he slept out on Whixhall Moss, a vast open common half a mile from the farm, consisting mainly of peat. Many of the villagers had their own little plot where they used to cut the peat, dig it up and then put it in piles to dry. This used to supply them with a pleasant-smelling stock of free fuel for the winter.

CHAPTER 16

VETERINARY WORK

When our lovely young brown and white Ayrshire heifers came down from Scotland, they all had magnificent, shapely, pointed horns on them. In any herd there has always got to be a boss cow or leader. As all our 60 animals had come from different herds, they proceeded to sort one another out. If not checked, this can be very expensive for the farmer. One year the champion Ayrshire cow at the London Dairy Show was killed by a spiteful neighbour. Not only will they attack each other, but they are quite capable of using their horns on the herdsman when he is trying to chain them up for milking.

I had a consultation with my veterinary surgeon, who strongly advised de-horning. My herdsman, George, was all for it. I lay awake at night wondering what to do! They looked superb with their gleaming horns and I hated the thought of de-horning them. Eventually, common sense prevailed and I told my vet to go ahead.

I couldn't bear to be there for the act and it was with a heavy heart that I drove home that night from my optical practice. I opened the shippon door, and there were all my beautiful cows, hornless, and with the tops of their heads covered in blood. A huge pile of horns lay outside the shippon. Tears filled my eyes and cascaded down my cheeks. I was too miserable that night to appreciate the lovely supper that Sheila had prepared for me.

The herd were not long in getting over their ordeal, and in two weeks' time were all healed up and carrying on as if nothing had happened. They were certainly much quieter and easier to handle.

To the townsman, farming is traditionally a romantic and easy way of life, but the harsh reality is that sometimes it can appear barbaric.

From then on, all our calves were de-horned when they were a week old. It was quite a simple and painless procedure: a special electric iron with a heated metal ring is pressed on the horn bud before it starts to grow and this saves them the trauma of having to be de-horned when they are older. This method is now standard practice in most of the dairy herds throughout the country and has certainly saved a lot of injury, both human and bovine.

I was never happier than when I was on the farm, and even after a hard day in optics, as soon as I had eaten my supper I would be out in the fields during the summer months. It was a satisfying job in that you could see the results of your labours. If you had sown a field of corn, it was very exciting to see it starting to sprout. You could also see if you had made a good job of it, or not. The same thing with your stockbreeding. As the young calves grew into heifers, you could see whether as a result of your line breeding, they were getting more shapely udders and stronger rear legs. "A cow is as good as its legs," is the old adage.

In the winter I very often used to go into the shippon in the evening and enjoy myself clipping the rear of the cows, and washing their tails in large buckets of hot soapy water. My farming friends thought that I was mad, but I really got a lot of pleasure walking along the lines of cattle, and seeing them spotlessly clean and healthy.

All my cows were washed each day before milking, and a strip cup used to test the fore milk from each teat, to check that there were no signs of mastitis. Mastitis is an inflammation of the udder caused by flies and other insects, particularly during the summer.

If not promptly treated this can lead to the loss of a quarter, and of course greatly reduces the value of the animal. It is simply treated nowadays by injecting a tube of penicillin into the affected teat.

I am appalled when I see farming programmes on TV today. They are usually of big commercial herds, where the cows walk into overhead 'milking parlours' and the milker is standing in a passage below. The cows are usually filthy through sleeping out rough. They are unwashed, and simply have the milking clusters put straight on. They would have to be suffering from a very badly inflamed udder before any infection was noticed! I hate to think what we might be getting in our milk today.

During the summer, another thing one has to be on the alert for is Warble Fly. This fly burrows underneath the skin and can cause great distress if untreated. If we saw any tell-tale lumps, we used to douse their backs with mops impregnated with a special lotion. Sores and wounds were treated with sulphanilamide powder.

In a herd of cattle one has to be constantly alert for signs of ill health. If a cow detaches herself from the herd and stands in a corner by herself, there is probably something worrying her, and it needs to be investigated. A good herdsman will know immediately if a cow goes off her food or has colic. If a drench has to be administered, this is done by filling a hock or similar bottle with the necessary medicine, inserting your fingers into the cow's nostrils, and pulling her head back until the drench can be poured in.

As I have mentioned before, I took a short course on animal husbandry before going onto the farm and found it to have been invaluable, not only in saving vet's bills, but in being able to give instant treatment. As a cow gets older, her hooves become overgrown and if not attended to, she will quickly become lame. To deal with this problem, I bought a special pair of clippers, so that if we had a cow with overgrown hooves, we used to rope her, throw her and tie her legs together and then did the necessary trimming. If a cow got thrush between her hooves, we painted them with Stockholm tar.

I had a special room, where I used to keep all my medicinal supplies and instruments.

One day during the spring George the herdsman banged on our kitchen door in a great state.

"Ring the vet quick, one of the heifers has got over the fence into the kale and must have been gorging herself for hours. She's lying on her back with her feet in the air, and blown up like a balloon."

What to do! If I rang the vet he probably woudn't be in and it would all waste precious time.

With the fermenting gases in her stomach building higher and higher, if the pressure wasn't released quickly she would die.

I grabbed my trochar and canula and ran after George up the field. By this time all the farm hands were surrounding the heifer, which was lying quite motionless with her feet in the air and her eyes already glazed. Was I too late! I felt her pulse. No! She was still alive.

I had been taught what to do on my husbandry course, but it's a different matter putting it into practice when it's your own valuable beast.

The first thing to do was to get her in the right position, so I got all the men to roll her over so that she was lying on her stomach. A faint moan came out of her.

A trochar and canula, I should explain, is a bit like the old fashioned pea shooter, but with a dagger in the tube – the trochar being a hollow tube and the canula a sharp-pointed dagger which rests inside it.

To relieve the pressure, there is a crucial point on the animal's back into which the canula has to be driven – this releases the gases and the trochar is then inserted to keep the passage open.

With trepidation, I raised the dagger, prayed to God that this was the right spot and drove it through the tough hide as hard as I could. There was an immediate sound of escaping gases, as I quickly inserted the trochar, which had a wide lip at the top to prevent it from going in too far.

After a few minutes the heifer started to show signs of life, and it wasn't long before she was on her feet and wandering around as if nothing had happened.

With this little event I achieved a certain notoriety in the district and subsequently had several calls for help from worried neighbours.

CHAPTER 17

THE CARAVAN

*O*ld Bill eventually got his bungalow built, and I strolled over one evening to see how they were getting on. Yes – they had got a bathroom. But I'm sure they didn't know what to do with it.

I was invited to have a cup of tea and a piece of cake, so whilst this was being prepared I had a look around the room. Amongst other things there was a piano and a new three-piece suite. There were no brown paper patches on the walls, but believe it or not, the wall had been painted with bright yellow emulsion and the paint – instead of covering the whole wall – just covered the outline of the furniture. I wondered if I was old-fashioned and this was the new way of conserving energy.

We chatted for a while, for Old Bill was interested in what we had been doing with the various fields.

"I believe you are planting a rose garden in the yard! IT'S MUCK YOU WANT."

I nearly died of laughter. He'd certainly left plenty of it to clear up.

When Old Bill and his sister sold us the farm they had retained 10 acres on which they had built their bungalow. This field was at the far end of the farm, had access to one of the back lanes and didn't interfere with us in any way. Whilst they were waiting for the bungalow to be built they bought a luxury Berkeley Ambassador caravan to live in. It had all mod cons including slatted blinds, built-in radio and even a small coal fire.

When they eventually moved into their bungalow the caravan was of course redundant.

Bill had apparently been in touch with the firm who had supplied the van and they had offered to buy it back. I asked him how much they were prepared to pay. The price they had offered was about half of what it had cost new. It appeared to be a bargain, so I asked him if he would sell it to me instead.

When I told Sheila that I had bought a caravan she thought that I was mad.

I had suddenly had a brainwave – a caravan of this size with six berths would make an excellent holiday home and would save us renting accommodation.

By this time our son Richard was a boarder at a prep school, and Anne, our daughter, was away at Goudhurst College near Nantwich. Jane, our younger daughter, was still going to nursery school.

We just had to get away from the farm for an occasional break and also let the children have a glimpse of the sea. We decided to take the caravan down to Abersoch.

I contacted Ernest, my chemist friend on the Wirral, and asked him if he fancied doing a delivery trip with me to take the caravan down to Abersoch. Yes – he would love to come.

Ernest came over to Shropshire and spent the night with us. Early the next morning we hitched the 22ft caravan onto the back of the Land Rover and were on our way. We stopped at the Prince of Wales hotel in Betwys y Coed and had lunch and arrived in Abersoch at about 4.30pm. I had decided to locate the caravan on The Warren so I drove in through the gateway and enquired about a site. I was directed to an area where I would see a man called Harry, who would tell me where I could unload my caravan. Harry indicated a broad area, and told me to make my choice. I espied what I thought would be an ideal spot. It was up a steep bank and was secluded from the other sites. The problem was how to get my caravan up there! I got my wallet out.

"Do you think that you can get it up there, Harry?"

"It will be a hell of a job, but I'll try."

While Harry tried, Ernest and I visited the camp store and purchased a number of necessary items like buckets, water carriers, etc. We then went down to the town, had a few beers and a good dinner. We spent a very comfortable night in the caravan, which Harry had managed to put in my chosen site. We drove back to Shropshire the next day.

In those days The Warren was a happy-go-lucky site and we spent several enjoyable holidays there. Today it is a very different place, highly-organised and highly-priced, with enormous prefab-type caravans sitting on concrete slabs and surrounded by miniature gardens.

CHAPTER 18

ON THE WAY UP

When we had been on the farm for five years, we were beginning to see the fruits of our labours. By this time we were on mains electricity and, thank goodness, were able to dispose of our much-maligned diesel generating plant, although we did install a single cylinder Lister petrol engine, which would operate the milking machine in case of mains failure.

Arthur, our field man, had spent all of the winter months hedge-laying, so our fields were beginning to look quite spruce with their new leys and new galvanised steel gates. All the hedges had originally been in a terrible state – many were 15ft high and full of gaps.

Hedge-laying is a highly-skilled job and is very time consuming. It necessitates pulling the very tall branches down until they are about two feet from the ground, then making deep cuts in them so that they will stay in place. They are then intertwined and vertical stakes are driven in to hold them in position. The object is to have a good thick hedge with no gaps, which will provide shelter from the wind and keep the livestock safely in the field without having to resort to barbed wire.

Some of the hedges in England are a thousand years old and are teeming with wildlife but modern practice has been to dig them up to make larger fields producing larger crops. This is a practice with which I do not agree.

Arthur was an expert hedge-layer and it used to gladden my heart to see how our hedges were improving. Like all countrymen, Arthur loved a good gossip, and as a lot of our fields bordered the main road through the village, the laying did not always proceed as fast as I would have liked.

All the ditches had been dug out, and a lot of the old tile drains had been replaced by pipe drains. The tile drains consisted of upturned U-shaped terracotta tiles. Over the years the open bottom of these would get filled up, and become totally blocked. The average field is riddled with drains which ultimately channel surplus water into the ditches, and if they become blocked, large pools of water will form. The only way of locating the direction in which they run is to poke down into the soil with a pointed steel rod until you feel it hit a pipe.

The very earliest drains were called mole drains. These were formed by dragging a bullet-shaped tool underground which formed a passageway, similar to that made by a mole. These had their uses and were better than nothing, but were only semi-permanent.

Arthur was also an expert mole-catcher. When we arrived on the farm, the whole place was covered in molehills. We got tired of harrowing these down, so I used to give him a shilling for each mole that he caught. Each Saturday there was usually a long line of moles hanging on the barbed wire fence for me to count.

By now we had established an attested herd of sixty, and our milk yield and butter fats were amongst the highest in Shropshire. We were also running about 60 head of young stock, plus about 20 dairy calves The best of the young stock were sired by our Ayrshire bull and would ultimately take their place in the milking herd, or be sold as in-calf heifers. The remainder, sired by our Aberdeen Angus bull, would be sold for beef.

At this time, I usually kept Tuesdays free so that I could go to the weekly market at Shrewsbury. I would go in the Land Rover and if we had any pigs or calves for sale, I would hitch on the trailer and take them in that. I quite enjoyed going to the market and usually had a good solid roast beef lunch, washed down with a pint of bitter – that is after I had sold my stock! It was as well to attend the sale ring and keep up-to-date with the value of any stock that we might be likely to sell. I got to know all the dealers and their different ways of making a bid, so that I could soon tell if the bids were genuine or not. I never bought in any cattle or pigs from the market myself, as I was running a home-bred closed herd and did not want to risk bringing in disease. I would occasionally have the loan of a boar from my friend Ken Smith, so that I could cross-breed some of my sows which were related through my boar's bloodline.

Ken had a prize-winning herd of Ayrshires and a prize-winning herd of Large White pigs. He was of course a lifelong full-time farmer, had a model farm and had won all sorts of awards for good husbandry. The pearls of wisdom which he offered were always gratefully received.

CHAPTER 19

FREE SPECTACLES

About this time free spectacles for everyone were introduced into the National Health Service, and of course everybody wanted them. I already had two very busy optical practices and with limited staff didn't want any more business – however, I didn't have much choice. I found I was absolutely besieged.

My appointment book rapidly filled up to the extent that I couldn't offer a free appointment for three months. Life became hell: it was impossible to obtain a qualified assistant and all the prescription houses were completely overwhelmed. Once I carried out an examination, it would take at least another three months before there was any hope of the patient receiving their glasses.

It got to the stage where I daren't go out through the front door, for people would corner me in the street, shake their fists, and tell me that without their glasses they were unable to go to work and that their family was starving.

I did my best! I frequently worked a 12-hour day, and then had to drive 35 miles home to the farm.

Not only that, I had all the everyday worries of the farm to attend to and frequently had to get up in the middle of the night for a calving.

Sheila was able to come and help me on the odd occasion but

she had three small children to consider, and of course if she wasn't there it left the farm without a supervisor.

After about a year the novelty of free specs wore off a bit and also I managed to engage a qualified assistant. I began to breathe once again.

I made a lot of money, and so was able to further satisfy my craving for fast cars. Sheila said she didn't mind as long as I wasn't after fast 'wimmin,' so I quickly added a Sunbeam Rapier, a 3.4 and a 3.8 Jaguar to my list. These exotic toys considerably eased the pain of my daily journey, and of course being a farmer were allowable income tax 'perks'.

The sad part was that most of the money I earned in my optics was immediately swallowed up on farm equipment and improvements.

What could I do to make the farm self-supporting?

CHAPTER 20

EXPERIMENTAL POULTRY UNIT

Reading through the local newspaper I saw that the Government were dismantling a Polish wartime camp at Ellesmere, Shropshire, about ten miles away.

I thought it sounded interesting, so I went over to investigate. There were a number of huts available in good usable condition. They had brick walls, with steel-framed windows each side, and asbestos roofs. They also had a double door at one end and were about 100ft x 14ft in size. I can't remember how much they were offered at, but I know they were a definite bargain.

My immediate thought was that one would make an ideal deep litter house and we could start a poultry unit. The only snag was that they had got to be dismantled by the purchaser and carted away.

I went home and discussed it with the men. Could they conceivably dismantle a unit like that, transport it back to the farm and re-erect it? They thought it might be possible.

I thought the best thing was to take them over to Ellesmere so that they could see what they were taking on. So I bundled them into the car and over we went.

To my delight they were all for it.

With some trepidation I wrote out a cheque and became the

owner of one massive prefab.

It was at the end of the summer, and all our corn had been safely harvested, so apart from the daily milking and feeding of the livestock there were no urgent jobs to consider.

The morning milking was finished by 8am, and the afternoon milking was started by 4.30pm, so in between those hours the boys would have to get to Ellesmere, dismantle as much as possible, load it, and be back home by 4.30pm.

Each day whilst George was doing the milking, Arthur and Colin got everything ready for the journey. Our little grey Ferguson tractor was filled with diesel, and all the demolition gear loaded up, plus a large hamper filled with sandwiches, fruit and flasks of tea.

As soon as milking was finished, the cows were turned out to pasture for the day, and our three intrepid demolishers were out of the yard and on their way to Ellesmere.

They were like three kids being let out of school for the day – they absolutely loved it. I suppose it was the novelty of doing something different.

Arthur was the brains of the outfit and took charge of the demolition – no mean task as, of course, it all had to be done methodically, and if possible without any breakages.

They started off by first stripping the roof. Each day stacks of the sheets were loaded onto the trailer, numbered and brought back to the farm for storage. Once the roof was stripped they then had to dismantle the steel roof-supporting girders and the lighting. This was also loaded and brought home. Next came the brickwork, which was painstakingly dismantled a brick at a time. I don't think that they broke a single brick. The final items were the windows and doors. There were eight double windows, four each side, and two doors.

When they got back each night, whilst George was milking, Arthur and Colin would unload the trailer and carefully store the numbered parts.

The next problem, of course, was how to get it all re-erected. It is far easier to take things down than to put them up again. I needn't have worried. Arthur had got it all worked out, and don't forget, as I have previously mentioned, he had but very rarely been to school.

The first thing to be done was to install a nine-inch thick concrete floor, which had to be dead level. This required one hell of a lot of concrete, so we all had to buckle to and help. The building gradually started to take shape, and I was filled with admiration for our building team. All the windows were perfectly level, the brickwork was a work of art and even the overhead lighting worked.

The erection took about three months to complete, which was not too bad considering all the routine farm work that had to be fitted in as well. Two coats of paint inside and outside, and we had got a super 100ft x 14ft building for a fraction of the cost of building a new one. I had intended making this into a deep litter house and starting a poultry unit. However, things worked out rather differently.

My friend, Ken Smith, and his wife, May, came over one night to have dinner with us shortly after our building was completed. He was very impressed and wanted to know what I intended to do with it.

"I was thinking of turning it into a deep litter house, Ken."

"Oh, I wouldn't do that, Jack. Deep litter is a lot of work. You don't know which hens are laying and which are not. It is very unhygienic, and you will also find birds fighting and pecking one another. What's more, if you get just one bird with coccideosis, the whole lot will be affected. With a super building like this, I am sure that I could get you on a breeding experimental programme."

I pricked up my ears. This sounded interesting.

It transpired that there was a large firm of poultry breeders in Yorkshire who were experimenting with all sorts of different crosses. Their aim was to produce birds with good health and high egg-laying potential. Apparently, they were on the lookout for reliable people with suitable facilities, who would take over the birds as day-old chicks and monitor every stage of their life. Ken was himself just starting a very large experimental unit for this firm, so he got in touch with them and put my name forward.

Yes – they would be interested, on Mr Smith's recommendation, to consider me as a suitable person to take part in their project. A meeting was arranged and a representative of the firm arrived to inspect our set-up. First of all, in order to record the number of eggs laid by each bird, it would be necessary to install a battery unit with a single cage for each bird. He thought that my building was ideal and calculated that it would be possible to run a 600-bird unit. The birds would all be supplied free, as day-old chicks. They would each have two wing bands on them with their individual numbers, and I would have to supply the firm with a weekly report on their progress (i.e. if any bird died, and if so, what was the cause, such as overlaying, pecking, coccideosis etc.), and I would have to return the appropriate wing band.

This was obviously going to be a major project, as it would involve the purchase of 600 cages, plus all sorts of ancillary gear. Sheila and I did a few calculations, and worried as to whether it was a feasible project. First of all, we had not had much experience of poultry-keeping. We had previously only run a couple of dozen hens on free range, none too successfully. Secondly, it would involve a considerable amount of clerical work, keeping all the weekly records and communicating with the breeders, and thirdly, our three regular workers were all fully employed and would not have the time for looking after 600 hens. It would mean, therefore, that we would have to engage another member of staff.

I went to see my bank manager in Ellesmere Port, who was a great personal friend. Fortunately, he thought that it would be a very useful and regular source of income, once we could get it running. He was quite agreeable to increase our overdraft to pay for all the equipment we should require.

We decided to have a go. Once having signed the contract with the breeders, we set about preparing our premises for accommodating 600 day-old chicks. These were due to arrive in March and in North Shropshire, March can be very cold, with frost and even at times, snow on the ground. The chicks would have to be adequately protected from the cold on arrival, or they would all perish the first night.

Around our farmyard we had a whole series of wagon sheds where the hay rakes, tine harrows, roller, carts, and so on were normally kept. These would have to be dragged out and put at the back of our seven-bay Dutch barn, until we could make other arrangements. The next thing was to convert one of the sheds into a warm, draught-free place for the chicks. The first step was to build a front to the shed with door access. We then erected a wooden roof scaffolding, which had tightly packed bales of straw laid on top to retain the heat.

There were various ways of rearing day-old chicks. Some methods consisted of electric fans blowing warm air down onto them. This we considered to be too risky, as there was always the possibility of a power cut. Some of the big breeders who used this method had a standby electric plant to fall back on. Another method was to have solid floor units with a central lamp to provide the heat. The disadvantage of this was that the chicks nearest to the lamp could get crushed, while the ones furthest away could get chilled.

The system we eventually decided on was warm floor brooders, which consisted of a well-insulated galvanised steel roof with ventilation holes in. Underneath there was a wire mesh on which the chicks perched, underneath the wire mesh were a series of oil lamps which provided the heat.

Provided they were re-filled with paraffin each day, and their wicks were kept trimmed, they were regarded as pretty well foolproof. Food and water was provided on each side of the brooder.

We installed a number of steel supported ex-WD trestle tables and mounted six large brooders of this type on top of them.

As the great day for the arrival of the chicks approached, I decided that we had better engage someone to look after them. Enter Margaret, our poultry girl. Margaret was the daughter of Ernest Green, a portly amiable character who had worked for the local builders. Ernest was on the point of retiring, as he suffered from terrible attacks of asthma.

We wanted a double garage building, so we took pity on Ernest and engaged him to build it 'in his own time'. Somehow he ended up as another permanent member of our staff, as we always seemed to be either redecorating or building something.

Margaret was a very pretty golden-haired, bubbly sort of girl, and it was a delight to hear her singing away in the battery house – but that was some time in the future.

Before the chicks were due to arrive, we lit all the lamps in the brooders for three days to warm everything up and check that they were working properly.

The day when the chicks did arrive was, of course, bitterly cold. Unfortunately on this particular day I had a full day's appointments booked for me in Ellesmere Port, so I was full of apprehension as I drove into the farmyard. How many of the chicks would be dead!

I opened the door of the shed and went inside. The first thing I was aware of was how warm it was – the heat from all the lamps and 600 chicks had certainly made a difference.

I lifted one of the brooder lids and peeped inside. What a sight met my eyes! Dozens of little golden haired balls of fluff were cheeping away and fighting each other for a place at the feeding troughs. I lowered the lid and breathed a sigh of relief. So far, so good! Everything seemed to be going according to plan.

I closed the door and hurried across the yard, out of the freezing cold and into the warm kitchen, where my supper, a big roaring fire and my wife awaited me.

I found that the breeders had delivered to us a few more chicks than the 600 we had agreed upon, presumably to compensate for any casualties. And of course there would be casualties, mostly due to overlaying. In an attempt to keep warm, for the first few days the chicks would pile up on top of each other to sleep, and this would result in the ones at the bottom being squashed flat and asphyxiated. Overall we didn't do too badly for our first attempt, and didn't have to send back too many wing bands.

After their first few weeks in the brooders, the next step was to get them out into the field in hay boxes. These consist of wooden boxes, with apex roofs and slatted floors. The roof, as the name would suggest, was stuffed with hay or straw, which acted as insulation, and conserved the body heat from the chickens. Attached to the end of each box was an 8ft wired-in run. We had lines of these boxes stretching out across the field. The theory was that the birds would have a constant supply of fresh grass to peck at, while their droppings would be spread evenly over the field. This worked very well in practice and there was a marked improvement in fertility over the area covered by the units. The boxes had strong handles at each end, and were moved en bloc at least once a day, so that gradually the whole field was fertilised. Soon our little balls of fluff were growing into fine young pullets and were rapidly filling their hay boxes.

The next stage was to get them onto free range. To accommodate them we had a number of 10ft-long huts constructed. These were mounted on wide-section metal wheels, so that they could be moved by the tractor every few days. Each night the birds had to be locked in their houses to protect them from predators.

We used to wait until it was nearly dark and then Sheila and I would traipse across the field to shut up the various huts. It sounds easy but invariably we would find that there were awkward characters which had decided to stay out for the night. Some would be perched up in the trees, while others would have burrowed right underneath the house. It used to be my job, because I had longer arms, to lie flat on my face partly beneath the house and try to grab their legs. Very often it seemed to be blowing a gale and pouring with rain, and my language as I dragged out the squawking birds was quite choice.

As I let go, they would fly into the air and Sheila would have to catch them on the wing. We developed quite a technique. They got plenty of exercise, as did we, and were in prime condition when they were approaching the point-of-lay stage.

The next step forward was when we really had to start paying out our hard-won cash. We would have to fill our big poultry house with wire mesh cages, one for each bird. We had been around and visited various cage manufacturers, and eventually decided that it would be best to get a local firm from Shrewsbury to do the job. The whole set-up looked horribly complicated and we thought that in the event of any breakdown we would have someone on the spot to put things right.

A fully-automatic system was terribly expensive, but after due consideration we decided that it would probably be worthwhile from the labour-saving point of view. We gave the local firm the order and prayed that the installation would be complete before the birds started laying.

We were lucky. The firm that we had chosen had only commenced trading six months previously. When they knew that this was going to be a showpiece experimental unit, they pulled out all the stops and even offered us a small discount if, once the unit was in commission, we would allow them to bring the occasional prospective customer to view it.

The cages were triple-tiered with wire floors, which were set at a slight slope so that the eggs would run down to a tray at the front, where there were two cards, one giving the wing band number, and other details of the bird. The second card was marked with the days of the week and the egg yield would be entered and totalled at the end of the week. Below the wire mesh, there was a solid reinforced glass floor, on to which the droppings fell. Along the front of the cages there was a continuous feeding trough, and underneath there was a water trough, so that the birds had a constant supply of fresh water.

The feeding and cleaning apparatus was a complicated affair and consisted of a system of scrapers and meal bins, all operated by electric motors twice a day. The meal bins, one for each tier, were filled with meal from a big barrow situated at the front door. As the meal bins moved along in one direction, and deposited meal into the troughs, the scrapers, by means of a wire rope, would be pulled along the glass floors in the opposite direction, and deposit the droppings into a bin.

As the birds would be coming into lay during the cold dark winter months, it was necessary to install a comprehensive lighting system, which was controlled by time switches. This would turn the lights on at dusk until about 10pm, and switch on again about 6am.

The shed was of course beautifully warm due to the birds' body heat, and so the idea was to simulate as near as possible spring-like conditions.

Everything was now in order for the start-up of our experimental unit. Several of the birds had already started laying.

First of all, every bird was treated with a special de-lousing powder before it was put into its cage. If chickens are sleeping together in a big shed, they can become infected with little red blood-sucking mites. If left untreated this would cause great distress and seriously affect egg production.

The breeders came over to supervise the installation of the birds. They were housed in groups according to their breed and they all had special numbers (i.e. 101, 202, 404, etc.) in addition to their individual wing bands.

The breeders were highly delighted with our set-up, and complimented us on the condition of the birds and our low mortality rate. We had signed an agreement with them to record every detail of each individual bird, so it all had to be taken very seriously.

Margaret was very pleased to be put in charge of this special experimental unit and really took an interest in it. She was kept quite busy, collecting eggs and packing them, and marking off on the charts each day the number of eggs each bird laid. Don't forget, these were no ordinary hens, they were super birds, and very soon some of them started laying two eggs a day.

It took a few weeks to get the units working properly. We had water troughs overflowing, the meal not being distributed evenly, and on one memorable occasion, one of the scrapers broke loose and smashed four of the glass floors. We were glad that we had chosen a local firm for the installation. They were very good, came out the same day, and soon had everything working again.

The eggs were mostly spotlessly clean, unlike deep litter units where a large number have got to be washed. They all had to be graded – small, medium, and large, and were then put on trays and packed into large wooden boxes ready for collection by the Egg Marketing Board. Each week, I found that I had a time-consuming job recording the weekly tally for each individual bird and filling in the charts supplied by the breeders.

Fortunately the birds were a pretty healthy lot, so we didn't have many casualties to report. With the odd one which did succumb, I had to send a report saying what I considered was the cause of death and return its wing bands.

All in all, I was well pleased with our poultry unit. It was a constant source of interest and what was even more important, provided us with a regular income.

I was asked by friends unconnected with farming whether I thought it was cruel to keep birds in cages.

First of all, our birds were experimental breeds and the only way of knowing if they were an improvement on the standard Rhode Island Reds, Light Sussex etc, was to treat them as individuals. Each of them had a decent size cage to themselves, unlike commercial batteries, where birds were de-beaked and put three to a cage. That I do consider cruel – and I could not have kept birds in that way.

On the odd occasion when a bird escaped from its cage, we would find it frantically running around the hut and doing its best to get back to what it considered was its home – where it always had plenty to eat and drink, in company with its mates, and had not got to stand out in the rain or snow waiting for someone to throw down a handful of corn for which it had to compete with all its neighbours.

As far as the breeder was concerned, the laying life of the hens was about 10 months, and their egg production after that would not remain a commercial proposition. We were therefore at liberty to do what we liked with them. By this time we would have reared the next batch of birds to take their place. Most of them would be sold to a dealer from Manchester who supplied hotels and restaurants. Some of them were bought by the local smallholders for a low price. They were put out on free range and given a rest, after which they would start production once again.

CHAPTER 21

A DELAYED JOURNEY

In the spring the milking herd were turned out to grass, lay out overnight and only came in twice a day for milking. As an inducement to get them into the shippon, they were each given a ration of meal which was weighed and apportioned according to the quantity of milk they were producing.

They each had their name on a slate in front of their stall, and they always knew the right place to go.

We had two pedigree bulls, an Ayrshire and an Aberdeen Angus. The Ayrshire had by this time matured into a magnificent specimen and had his own comfortable quarters. Adult Ayrshire bulls can be particularly vicious, so it was considered unsafe to turn him out and leave him in a field on his own. In order that he should get some outside exercise we used the generally accepted method.

A heavy steel spike was driven in to the ground and a rod was linked to it so that it could turn in a circle. The bull was attached to the rod by a long length of chain which clipped onto his nose ring. By this means he could move around the circle and graze the fresh grass. He was moved twice a day and then returned to his shed for the night.

Ben, our other bull, was a Black Angus, a breed renowned for its beef. He was only a yearling but when mature he was going to be used on our poorer milkers in order to produce beefier store cattle.

He was considered to be safe to let out on his own for the whole of the summer, so had been turned out into a five-acre field which bordered the main road out of the village.

It was a gorgeous spring morning and much to my chagrin I had a full day's appointments at Ellesmere Port.

I got out my Jaguar and drove out of the farm gate. As I drove along the road and came alongside the five-acre field, what should I see but Ben down by the hedge, doing his best to escape to pastures new. I stopped the car, got out my stick, which I always carried, gave him a sharp whack on the nose and told him the error of his ways.

I turned to get back in my car and there, to my amazement, in the front passenger seat sat a portly well-dressed lady. It began to dawn on me who she was.

"What are you doing sitting there?'"

"I want to go for a ride."

"I can't take you for a ride – I'm on my way to work. Now will you please get out!"

"Shan't! I'm going for a ride with you!"

I was already 10 minutes late, and had over 30 miles to go. This of course was Emily, a well-known local figure and a bit of a nuisance in the village. She was slightly simple but perfectly harmless. She used to dress up each day, wander around and let herself into whatever house took her fancy. She would then sit herself down and demand tea.

She was a big powerful lady and I couldn't just drag her out. The only thing I could do was to reverse the car, take her back to the farm and let Sheila deal with her.

"There you are, you've had your ride, now go over there and into the house, and Sheila will make you a nice cup of tea and give you some chocolate biscuits."

It did the trick – she clambered out of the car and ambled over towards the house. Poor Sheila!

I certainly had to exceed the speed limit that day.

CHAPTER 22

THE MAD COW

When we were establishing our herd, the dealer Reg Roberts went to a lot of trouble to get us a well-matched lot of heifers down from Scotland. If we were dissatisfied in any way, we only had to give him a ring and they were exchanged without question.

We had one in-calf heifer which was really wild. When we thought she was due to calve we tried to bring her into one of the loose boxes. It was hopeless, every time we went near to her, she took off and charged around and around the field. Eventually Sheila saddled up Kerry and tried to herd her into the yard. She wasn't having any – she could run as fast as the horse, and eventually leapt over a five-barred gate to escape into another field. I rang up Reg.

"No problem, I'll be out in the morning and collect her."

True to his word, he arrived at 11 the next morning, towing a smart horse box behind his Humber Super Snipe. Inside was a replacement heifer.

Reg, of course, was an expert with cattle, and after an hour eventually cornered the wild one and got a rope around her neck. It took five of us to to get her into the trailer. Reg didn't want any more trouble and took her straight to the abattoir for slaughter. When she was opened up, a piece of barbed wire was found in her stomach.

No wonder the poor beast was demented.

CHAPTER 23

THE VILLAGE FETE

Cordy and Dennis Hockenhull, our next-door neighbours, were a great source of help and were unstinting with their advice if we had a farming problem which we couldn't solve. Their farm was slightly larger than ours and had been in the Hockenhull family for generations. Instead of selling their milk, they concentrated on making cheese and fed the whey to store pigs which they were fattening for market. They were not yet attested, so we had to double-fence all our adjoining fields to avoid our cattle coming into contact with theirs. They were wise, and were waiting until they could claim a subsidy for all the expenses involved in establishing an attested herd.

Cordy had also come from a long line of farmers and was typical of the efficient and hard-working farmers' wives.

It was the practice in those days that on marriage the husband was handed down a farm, while the wife's parents would provide the household goods and much of the livestock. It was a bit tough if you started farming without marrying a farmer's daughter. (Sorry, darling – I wouldn't swap you!)

The Hockenhulls had four children, two of whom, John and Keith, were in the same age group as Anne and Richard. Our younger daughter, Jane, was only a toddler at that time, but John and Keith and our two elder children were great friends, and they used to have the run of two farms in which to get up to mischief.

There was no anxiety about child molesters in those days and drug abuse was unheard of amongst children. The country lanes were relatively free of traffic, so the children used to trundle down to the village shop to spend their Saturday pocket money on sweets, lemonade and Tizer. They went birds-nesting and generally enjoyed themselves.

One day they decided that they could do with more sweets and lemonade than their pocket money would provide, so to implement their resources they hit on the idea of holding a Village Fete! Cordy got wind of this and was appalled.

"They can't do that and keep the money for themselves!" she said.

Somehow, the vicar heard that there was the possibility of a fete in aid of the Church funds.

"What delightful children you have, to think of working to provide money for the Church Restoration Fund!"

Little did he know what scheming and mercenary little wretches they were.

We were dumbstruck! We were landed with running a fete on our farm, with all the work and expense that would be involved. Oh well! As ever we would make the best of it. All our staff were delighted, as it appeared that the last fete in the village had been before the war.

They were very loyal and wanted to show all their friends how we had improved the farm. It was springtime, so most of the stock were out in the fields. All the sheds were swept and then scrubbed with disinfectant. The rose beds in front of the house were cleared of even the tiniest weeds, all the windows around the yard were freshly painted. Fred, the bull was groomed to perfection, and the big yard was hosed and scrubbed.

We managed to hire some brightly-coloured bunting and this was draped all around the yard. A long line of coloured electric lights was strung up on the side of the house. Trestle tables were borrowed from the Church Hall, covered with fancy tablecloths and a bring and buy stall was set up. Cordy was in charge of this as she had dozens of relatives, and also knew everyone in the village. My air gun was unearthed and a shooting range was put safely in place. There was a treacle toffee and lollipop stall, a cake stall and so forth. All sorts of simple games were laid out, such as throwing rubber rings over bottles of wine and beer, rolling pennies down a wooden shute onto a square board with numbers on, and of course there had to be a coconut shy and bowling for the pig which had been kindly donated by a neighbour.

We had a large open shed in the yard which was used for storing peat and coal. We cleared it and installed a barbecue.

The children were delighted with all this, and really entered into the spirit of things. They busied themselves printing notices which they distributed all around the district.

At the request of all the staff, we also decided to run a Barn Dance in the evening!

We had a large two-storey barn, the top floor of which was used for storing sacks of corn. The ground floor was full of cattle and pig meal. The men set to with a will, humping the heavy sacks up the steps in double quick time. The last trace of meal was removed from the floor, the ceiling swept of cobwebs and the walls were then whitewashed.

Margaret, our cheerful, golden-haired girl who was in charge of the poultry, had to give it all her approval. She was obviously greatly looking forward to the evening's entertainment. Calling "I won't be long!" she dashed over to her bike and went hell for leather down to the village store. True to her word, she was back within five minutes clutching an enormous packet of soap flakes which she proceeded to sprinkle all over the barn floor.

"There now, that will make it nice and slippery for the dancing!"

She was obviously going to be the 'Belle of the Ball.'

I had recently constructed a powerful tape recorder, so I made a tape of all the latest dance music, plus a selection of Old Tyme waltzes. The apparatus was set up on a shelf, ready for the grand opening

Sheila was kept busy making stacks of scones and fancy cakes. Cordy, our neighbour, who was also of course involved, was equally busy baking.

We had hoped, as it promised to be a warm and sunny day, that we could provide afternoon tea on the terrace outside the house, but according to Cordy, that would never do. Apparently the highlight for all the farmers' wives would be to get inside the house, have a good nose around and have a gossip about it afterwards. This presented some difficulty, as although the house was large, we would only be able to seat about 20 at a time and we would therefore have to have two sittings.

At last the great day arrived and, as hoped for, it was blue skies and sunshine.

The Fete was due to start at 2pm. Bill Wyatt, the managing director of the firm which constructed our borehole, and a great friend by now, had kindly agreed to run a hot dog stall. He was all dressed up in chef's apron and high white hat. He had in front of him a long table on which were piled stacks of rolls and trays of pork sausages.

Bill soon got an enormous charcoal fire going, and rows of sausages sizzling away.

The vicar and his wife appeared shortly after the opening and he decided to give a short speech of appreciation. Unfortunately, he chose to be within eight feet of our chef who was busily engaged stoking up his fire. Apparently the charcoal was beginning to get a bit low, so he was augmenting it with pieces of peat and bits of coal. The Vicar was just beginning to get in his stride, when there was an almighty bang, and a piece of red hot asbestos suddenly shot past his wife's ear. It must somehow have been amongst the bits of coal which Bill had just put on the fire

The Vicar was not amused and his speech became a very short one, much to our relief.

Apart from this little incident everything seemed to be going according to plan and it was nice to see all the happy smiling faces.

The afternoon tea was a great success, everyone enjoyed themselves and our girls were complimented on their baking.

The Barn Dance was run as a separate event and didn't start until 8pm. It attracted a very different group of people from the day's jollifications. All the village lads and their girl friends arrived – the girls were all dressed up in pretty party frocks, and the lads even managed a wash and clean shirts. The tape recorder was a very powerful one, and as it boomed out a programme of carefully selected dance music, the party soon got going.

Margaret took charge of the dancing and was putting the couples through all sorts of dances we had never heard of. We managed to get another volunteer to start up the barbecue again, and we donated a limited number of soft drinks and a barrel of beer. We finally brought the festivities to an end at 11pm.

The Fete made a profit of £300 and was voted a roaring success. The Vicar was highly delighted and we received the usual letter of thanks.

We felt that our small entrepreneurs deserved some recompense, so we presented each of them with a large tin of toffees.

CHAPTER 24

WORKING DAYS

Apart from our yearly crops of hay and silage, we also grew about ten acres of kale. This was used as a standing crop for feeding the cattle in the autumn, before the ground got waterlogged. We used to erect an electric fence to divide off small sections of the kale each day for them to graze.

Our other main crops were wheat and oats. This was at the end of an era, before combine harvesters became popular and greatly reduced the labour of harvesting.

When the corn was ripe, it was cut with a binder as described earlier. The sheaves of corn were then left to dry out for a few days by propping them up into stooks of about six. They were then loaded onto the carts and brought back to the Dutch barn, where they were stacked until they reached the roof. This again was a highly skilled job – they were stacked in rows with the ears pointing inwards. If this was not done properly, the whole bay could topple over. After a month or two of drying in the barn, the great day arrived when the gigantic threshing machine rolled into the yard. This was a really fearsome apparatus, comprising the machine itself, which was mostly made of wood and had all sorts of chutes, levers and pulleys sticking out of it. Then there was the elevator or moving platform, and finally the baler. The whole contraption was pulled by an enormous single-cylinder diesel John Deere tractor.

Whilst the farm men were finishing the milking and feeding the calves, the threshing machine crew were sorting out all the bits and pieces and connecting up the great long belts which joined the machine to the tractor power take-off. Finally everything was ready to start threshing. It would be about 8.30am.

When the 'great beast' was started up, the clatter and banging, smoke and dust was like something out of Dante's Inferno.

First of all, there had to be two men with pitch forks on top of the stack – these were called the pitchers. It was their job to drag out the tightly-packed sheaves and pitch them onto the moving platform which fed them to the thresher. Another man was stationed below to cut the strings as they came down. A fourth man was at the hopper, where the corn came out and filled the sacks. It was his job to tie up the full sacks and put them ready for the fifth man, the tough guy, who would load the heavy sacks onto his back, and carry them up the barn steps to the loft. Meanwhile a sixth man would be catching the bales of straw as they came out and stacking them in one of the other bays.

I was one of the two pitchers. It did not seem too bad a job when I first started, but by the time it was 6pm, it was as much as I could do to lift the pitchfork!

It always amazes me how tough the average farm worker is. In the main they appear to be of quite modest physique but they will cheerfully, in harvest time, work for 12-hour stretches hurling bales of hay on the end of a pikel onto the waiting carts, and think nothing of it.

When the bottom of the stack was reached, all the farm cats and dogs gathered around expectantly. You could never tell what had made its nest there, but it usually contained an assortment of mice and rats, which bolted in all directions, hotly pursued by the cats and dogs.

We had the threshing outfit with us for three days. Fortunately I had the excuse of fully-booked appointments in my optical practice for the next two days, so another character took my place. I can't say that I was sorry, as I felt absolutely knackered.

CHAPTER 25

NIGHT OUT

I was fortunate in having a cheerful and willing gang of workers, so thought that Belle Vue at Manchester could provide a good evening's entertainment.

The afternoon milking had to be done before we could leave, but we started an hour early, and everyone mucked in so that we were in reasonable time to start our journey to Manchester.

There were six of us altogether, so I piled them all into the Land Rover and we roared off in high spirits.

Belle Vue is – or was – a great spot for a good night out. First of all there was a gigantic fun fair with a big dipper, all sorts of rides and dozens of side shows. There were also restaurants, fish and chip stalls, pubs, a boxing booth and an all-in wrestling show.

We were all feeling hungry after the long drive, so we went into one of the restaurants. I told the lads that expense was no worry, so they all ordered enormous meals, washed down with pints of beer.

Feeling suitably refreshed after a visit to one of the numerous pubs, we did the rounds of the big dipper and most of the rides on the fairground. We also tried our hands at the coconut shies and the shooting range, where George won a large teddy bear.

I happened to notice that the all-in wrestling show was about

IT'S MUCK YOU WANT!

to start, so I asked the lads if they would like to go. There was unanimous approval for my suggestion. I managed to get seats so we all trooped in and eagerly awaited the opening bout.

At that time all-in wrestling was very popular and all the top names were on the programme, including Mick McManus and the three Yorkshire wrestling brothers, Jack Pye, Harry Pye and Bully Pye.

It's a well-known fact that most of the bouts are faked, but nevertheless the wrestlers are obviously highly-trained and supremely fit athletes, and seem able to withstand punishment which would put the average man in hospital for a year.

Mick McManus was known for bending the rules, and of course took on an enormous negro who was about twice his size. For two rounds it looked as if the negro was going to kill Mick, but Mick was an extremely clever wrestler and in the third round he suddenly came to life, as always managing to get the winning fall.

The second bout was a double event, Harry and Bully Pye against a couple of tough-looking Spaniards.

The bout ran its normal course until the third round, when Harry and Bully were both on the floor, with the Spaniards howling for their blood and doing their best to get a submission.

This was too much for Jack Pye, who was supposedly a ringside spectator. He jumped from his seat, vaulted over the top rope, grabbed a Spaniard in each gigantic hand and knocked their heads together. Pandemonium broke out and he was eventually dragged out of the ring. In the meanwhile Harry and Bully had regained their feet, leapt to the attack on the Spaniards and won the fight.

No doubt it had all been rigged but it was still quite entertaining.

When we came out of the booth it was after 11pm so we decided to call it a day. They all scrambled into the Land Rover and we started on the long run home.

Fortunately I had not imbibed like the rest of them, so I didn't feel too bad about the driving, although I must admit I was feeling pretty sleepy by the time I had dropped them all off and finally pulled into the farmyard at about 1am.

CHAPTER 26

SEARCH FOR A NEW HOBBY

Now that the farm was running like clockwork, we had a bit more time to take stock of where our life was drifting.

When we looked back, we were amazed at our audacity – we had been full of the enthusiasm of youth and could only see the Golden Gate at the end of our dream.

We had abandoned a comfortable home with every luxury, left all our friends and migrated to a flea-ridden house with no water, no electricity and no sanitation, taken on an enormous overdraft, and I had a 70-mile journey most days to get to work to provide the money to keep the farm going.

We were obviously besotted with the thoughts of green fields, blue skies and the scent of new-mown hay.

But it didn't take long for the illusion to dim somewhat.

We'd had two luxurious bathrooms at our old home. The only way of getting a bath when we first arrived on the farm was to heat a tin bath full of water with a flame gun and then drag it into the kitchen in front of the old kitchen range.

After 10 years of really hard work, worry and deprivation all this had changed. We had arrived at the Golden Gate, and once again we had a six-bedroom house, with two bathrooms, a totally new dining room with a sapele mahogany floor and stone archways leading to a cocktail bar.

The farm itself had had a hell of a lot of money spent on it – money which I had earned in my optical practice. It was now in tip-top condition and was just about supporting itself.

But what about me and the family?

The family were growing up. Anne, our eldest daughter, had been going to a little private school in Whitchurch and she then went as a full-time boarder to Goudhurst College, near Nantwich. Our son Richard, who was slightly younger, was at Hampton House School at Tarporley, where he was being coached for the entrance exam for Malvern College.

All this private education of course had to be paid for, but as I have mentioned the farm was no longer a financial drain and we could now afford a full-time girl in the house to relieve Sheila of all household chores.

It was time for us to start and relax a bit.

We had up to now used all our energy in reorganising the farm and training our staff so that they could run things without constant supervision.

We wanted a hobby which all the family could join in. We had already sailed with some friends at Newquay and thoroughly enjoyed it. Sailing – that's what we would do!

There was a mere near to us, but really it was too small and was surrounded by trees and dense undergrowth, so most of the time you just sat there getting more and more frustrated by lack of wind.

The nearest practical place to go sailing was on the river at Chester, so we drove over there one Sunday afternoon to investigate.

There were a number of small multicoloured craft on the river, which seemed to vary in size and appeared to have different insignia on their sails. Some had the shape of a heron, others a bell, and there were various other emblems. It was all a bit mystifying.

There was a nice little clubhouse on the site, so we thought the best thing was to go inside and see if we could get any useful information.

There was a bar at one end of the room, the usual place where people like to talk, so we wandered over and introduced ourselves to a couple who looked as if they might be friendly.

"Good afternoon, I'm Jack Orrell, and this is my wife, Sheila. We are complete strangers to sailing, so wondered if you can give us some information on the subject."

"Sure! No problem! What do you want to know?"

"First of all, is membership of the club open to anyone?"

"Yes – if you are interested we would be delighted if you would like to join. The club hasn't been open for long, and we are looking for new members."

"We noticed that there appear to be different classes sailing – what do the marks on the sails mean?"

"The boats with the heron on the sail are Herons and the ones with the bell are GPs, or 'general purpose' 14-footers. Those are the two main classes which are sailed here. The Herons are a good beginner's boat, but they're not as fast as the GP. If you have a family, you would probably be best off with a GP, as they can easily carry four people."

"The dinghies outside appear to be racing – is this a regular feature here?"

"Oh yes, we hold races on Saturday and Sunday, and sometimes on Thursday evenings. At the moment we haven't got sufficient boats of one class to run a class race, so we have to use a handicapping system."

We thanked our new friends for all the information they had given us and left them alone to their drinks.

Once outside, we marvelled at the dexterity with which the dinghies were being handled.

By this time the wind had freshened considerably and the two people on board were perched up on top of the deck and hanging out over the side, their heads nearly in the water, in what appeared to be a desperate attempt to keep the boat upright.

It all looked very exciting and we wondered if we would ever be able to master the technique to control one of these lively beautiful toys.

The next day Sheila went into Whitchurch, to W H Smith, and bought a book on dinghy sailing. By the time I got home that evening she had already read a few chapters and was full of enthusiasm for the project.

"It's certainly not as easy as we first thought. Even when we've learnt to sail, there seem to be all sorts of techniques to make the boat go faster, and if we ever become expert enough to take part in races, there are pages and pages of racing rules to master."

We thought about it a great deal and wondered what would be the best way to start.

By coincidence I happened to see an advert in the *Ellesmere Port Pioneer* for a sailing dinghy.

It didn't specify what class it was, but sounded very cheap and also had its own trailer. I suggested that the first thing was to learn to sail, and as it would require some considerable experience before we were good enough to take part in any races, it didn't really matter what sort of boat we started off in.

I discussed the matter with my friend Bill Wyatt, who I discovered had built himself a GP14 from a kit.

"Well, Jack, I think it's worth having a look at this boat – it's cheap and could very well do you for a start. After all you may find that you and Sheila don't like sailing."

The next Saturday I rang up to see if the boat was still for sale. "Yes! It's still for sale and I shall be in all afternoon."

I collected Bill in my 3.8 Jaguar which had a towing hitch on the back.

The address we were given was in the Birkenhead district. When we eventually found the house it was about 5pm.

The dinghy appeared to be in quite good condition. It was home-constructed, 14ft long and somewhat like a GP in appearance only heavier. It had a rather clever trailer-cum-launching trolley included in the deal.

Bill thought it would suit our present needs, so I bought it.

The owner was quite a sailing enthusiast and intended building a larger boat.

We were invited in to tea, so it was 7.30pm before we hitched the boat onto the back of the Jag and started our journey homewards.

By the time we arrived at Broxton, which was approximately half way, Bill was apparently feeling a bit thirsty, so we decided to call at the Egerton Arms.

The Egerton Arms at that time was run by Terry Warburton. The whole of the Warburton family were patients of mine, and the 'Arms' was a regular port of call for me on my way home each night.

Friday night was a special night, when a little gang of us with Jaguars used to meet and swop yarns. Terry himself had a 3.4 Jaguar and was a motoring fanatic. He has now moved on, and owns Ruthin Castle, runs mediaeval banquets and has a Ferrari as one of his cars.

It was now closing time, and of course it was pitch dark before we emerged. With 'gassing away' we had quite forgotten that we were towing a boat, and there were no lights on the trailer. Not to worry! Terry darted inside and emerged with two electric torches and a couple of pairs of red socks, presumably belonging to his children, which we wrapped round the lenses and tied on to the rear of the trailer. This was, of course, in the good old days when there was little traffic and breathalizers hadn't been heard of. We once more headed for home. By the time we had got to Whitchurch, Bill decided that he was ravenously hungry. By this time, of course, all the pubs were closed for the night. This did not appear to be a problem for Bill. "Just pull in here, Jack." This was apparently Bill's local and he was almost one of the family. He strode up to the front and banged on the door. There was the sound of various bolts being withdrawn and we were inside. Bill made straight for the kitchen, where there was a giant refrigerator. He pulled out two huge steaks and flung them onto the grill which was still glowing from the evening's cooking. The landlord, by this time, had entered into the spirit of things and dished up a few chips, so that in no time at all we were indulging in a sumptuous repast. I rang up Sheila to say that we were on our way, but I had not counted on a midnight feast!

Bill was a real night owl and if you went out with him you never knew at what time you would arrive home. He lived in Whitchurch, so I drove him to his house and waited to see him safely in. He tried his key in the lock. No go! The door had been bolted and he was locked out.

Bill's house was a large detached building and at the front there was a balcony outside the bedroom window. This was fronted by an attractive lattice-work of wrought iron, the top section of which formed a row of *fleur de lys*. Bill's immediate reaction was that if he were to get a bed that night, he would have to climb up to the balcony and get in through the French windows. He had, apparently done this many times before, so he knew where the footholds were. Everything went well until he reached the top, when unfortunately one of the *fleur de lys* got stuck in the fly of his pants. The resultant kerfuffle as he tried to release himself woke Pam, his wife, who appeared in her nightgown, grabbed him by the scruff of his neck and hauled him up, saying "Come on up, dear!" I beat a hasty retreat.

Sheila's parents were retired and had gone to live in Paignton in Devon. We decided to go down and spend a week there.

"We may as well take the boat with us," I said.

"But we don't know the first thing about sailing yet! Hadn't we better have some sailing lessons before we go out on our own?" was Sheila's response.

"There's water at Paignton. Let's take it with us and see how we get on!"

We hitched the boat on and began the long haul down south. Pulling a trailer considerably lengthened the time of our journey, due to the speed restriction. When we arrived at my in-laws' bungalow, we unhitched the boat, put it in the garden and forgot about it for a couple of days.

Apparently there was a harbour at Paignton, so we thought that would be the best place to launch. We arrived at the harbour, unhitched the trailer and boat, wheeled it to the water's edge and then had to think of what to do next!

First of all, the mast had to be erected. It was a heavy wooden mast, and it took quite a lot of heaving and straining before we eventually got it up. It was, of course, very unstable and needed to be supported by some wires, namely a forestay and two shrouds. There ensued a frantic search in one of the sail bags for the shackles required to hold the 'wires' to the deck. We finally got the boat in the water, and fixed the rudder on. We then tried to raise the sails. We got the jib on all right, but when it came to the mainsail, not knowing the first thing about it, we hoisted it upside down! Naturally, our antics had not gone unnoticed and there was quite a sizeable audience of 'gawpers' on the promenade above us. The next problem was that the main halyard had jammed in its track. There was nothing for it but to take the mast down again in order to free it. By the time that we had re-erected the mast and got the mainsail up the right way, we found that the water in the harbour had started to ebb, and we were left high and dry. We had no option but to down sails and mast and drag the boat back onto the promenade. So ended our first attempt at sailing. It certainly made us realise that we had a great deal to learn. My mother-in-law said that they would keep quiet about their relations with a boat!

When we returned home, we decided that we had better join the Chester Sailing Club and see whether we could get a bit of

SEARCH FOR A NEW HOBBY

tuition. As I mentioned before, Bill had built himself GP14 and had sailed it a few times on a small lake near Whitchurch. Always game for any new adventure, we had no difficulty in persuading him to join the club as well.

The first thing to do was for one of us to learn to helm, i.e. to steer the boat. It was decided that I should be the guinea pig. There were plenty of people in the club who were only too anxious to help, so it was not long before I was able to rig a boat reasonably quickly and, in a light wind, steer it without hitting anybody. Once having got the basics right, it was just a matter of practice to get the feel of the thing and to be able to sail in a blow without capsizing. Capsizing is a regular hazard in dinghy sailing and nothing to be afraid of if you know what to do. You simply swim from under the sail which is in the water, round to the other side of the boat, stand on the centre board, grab the deck and pull. The boat will then come upright. Most boats at that time had blown up air bags in them to stop them from sinking. Later models had built-in buoyancy.

Now that I was reasonably confident, Sheila joined me as crew and had control of the jib sheets and the centre plate. By this time we had really got the sailing bug. We realised that if we were going to take it up seriously and learn to race, then our cheap original craft would have to be replaced by something like a GP14.

We decided to have a boat built, and with this in mind we went to see Sills, a firm in Liverpool, which at that time was specialising in GP14s and was producing boats sailed by the class champions. We were very impressed by the attention to details and the superb finish of their boats, so we put in an order. It was about three months before we heard that *Tamba* was ready for collection. When we took her to the club, all the members were green with envy. With her snow-white sails, pale blue sides and gleaming mahogany deck, she was indeed a thing of beauty.

At this time there was a medical student named Barry in the club. He was about 19 years of age, and was a sailing fanatic. He was extremely bright and knew all the sailing rules backwards. Barry did not have a boat of his own, so I asked him if he would race *Tamba* with me as crew, and teach me the racing techniques and intricate racing rules. He was apparently a member of one of the Firefly racing teams when at university, so whilst he was on holiday it would be an excellent opportunity for me to get some expert tuition.

Sailing on the River Dee could be very frustating, as there were frequent wind shifts due to the trees which lined the banks and there was also generally a strong tide running. This was marvellous training – it meant that I would get first-rate experience, as racing was taken seriously and no quarter was given. If you are on Port tack and your opponent is on Starboard, if you don't get out of his way and he has to alter helm to avoid you, you are disqualified and have to retire immediately. This is just a simple example – there are many complicated situations which can arise and have to be settled in protest meetings.

Once I had got the feel of the boat and became a proficient helm, I was absolutely sold on sailing and could not get enough of it. Sheila was also enthusiastic and was more than happy to join me as crew. A good crew is nearly as important as the helmsman, but doesn't have the responsibility of working out the racing tactics or the heart-throbbing moments of near-misses.

Whenever it was possible to leave the farm, we went over to Chester and took part in the racing. After a couple of years we began to think that pleasant enough though it was, river sailing, with 'flukey' winds, made it difficult to reach the full potential of which a boat was capable. We started to look for fresh fields of adventures. This was not too easy. The venue had to be within a reasonable travelling distance from the farm. We got to hear that Lake Bala was just becoming a centre for sailing and that a club was starting there. We went over to investigate and found that there was a nucleus of enthusiasts there who sailed a number of different classes of dinghies. They mostly came from the Wirral and Manchester areas, so their sailing was confined to weekends. Bala was a superb location, as the lake was huge, and we could see that there were great possibilities once the club became fully organised.

We had not really had a great deal of use out of our caravan at Abersoch as it was so far away, so we decided to sell it, buy a smaller one and try to find a site for it at Bala. Our aim in doing this was that we would be able to spend alternate weekends there and enjoy both a restful weekend and freer and more enjoyable sailing.

We bought a Welton 15ft caravan, and before taking it to Bala, decided that we would take it down to the Caravan Club site at the Crystal Palace in London. Our three youngsters had never been to London, so we thought that it would be an economical way of showing them some of our historical heritage.

I hitched the van onto the back of the Jag and began the long haul down to London. It had been a few years since I had driven in the capital and things were not quite as simple as they once were. To get to the Crystal Palace site it was necessary to negotiate Piccadilly Circus – not the easiest spot, when towing a caravan! Unfortunately, unbeknown to us, General de Gaulle was visiting the capital, and somehow we found ourselves at the front of his procession. There were guards of honour lining both sides of the road and as we drove through they seemed to be holding their breath to make room for us. We managed eventually to extricate ourselves and find the caravan site. This proved to be excellent and was very well managed, with hot showers and so on.

The next day we were up bright and early and were looking forward to seeing the sights. Unfortunately Jane, our youngest, complained of not feeling well by the time we reached Marble Arch, and was feverish. Sheila thought that the best thing to do was for me to take Anne and Richard into town on my own, as it would have been a pity to have spoiled their day as well. We three clambered onto one of the famous red double-decker buses, and were soon in the centre of Town.

The first thing that they wanted to see was, of course, the Tower of London, with the famous Traitor's Gate, the Crown Jewels and more than anything, the dungeons! This occupied the morning and by 12.15pm they were howling for food.

I wanted to give them a treat, so thought it would be a good idea to let them see what a high-class hotel was like. The Piccadilly Hotel was my choice, so we trooped in there. The head waiter showed us to a table and they gazed in awe at the enormous menu which was put in front of them. I had noticed when we went in that there was a *table d'hôte* lunch on offer, so we decided to have that. Our first course was a delicious soup, followed by the dish of the day, which was roast beef. Our waiter was intrigued that I had got a couple of youngsters with me, and no doubt puzzled by our less than immaculate attire. It was quite difficult trying to get dressed in a small caravan occupied by five people. He possibly thought that I was an eccentric aristocrat. Anyway, our waiter could not do enough for us. It was not just any old roast beef that was dished up onto our plates. Oh no! this was a 'posh' hotel. The waiter arrived pushing an enormous stainless steel trolley. He rolled back the lid, and inside was half a side of beef. The kids looked in awe as he produced a vicious-looking knife, which he then proceeded to waft backwards and forwards across the sharpening steel. He asked them if they were feeling hungry. They sure were! He hacked off three pieces each for them. "Surely you can't eat all that!" I said. They got stuck in and there was no question of it being too much. It was certainly was the most delicious, tender beef that I had ever tasted. The next problem was to choose a sweet. There was a choice of ten, including four ice creams. They had difficulty in making up their minds when faced with such a selection, but eventually they decided on the ice creams. When these arrived, they were enormous and had whole bananas sticking out of the top of them. It certainly was a meal to remember, and they even talk about it to this day – more than 40 years later!

When we came out into the lounge, I saw that there was a theatre booking agency there. Why not see if I could take them to a matinée of a London show? I had given the head waiter a substantial tip, so I approached him and asked if he could use his influence to secure me three tickets. The show I had chosen was *West Side Story*. The head waiter was in conference with the ticket agency, and after a few moments he returned and asked if I would like orchestra stalls. There were just three tickets available! It was way above the price I had intended to pay, but I really wanted it to be a day to remember, so I agreed.

You will never believe it. We had not only got orchestra stalls for the best show in town, but we were on the front row. Anne and Richard were absolutely thrilled to see one of the all-time 'greats' at such close quarters.

When we eventually got the caravan to Bala, I managed to secure a site at the south end of the lake and we left our GP14 at the north end of the lake, which was where the racing took place. We had to surround our caravan with barbed wire to protect it from the horns of the store cattle which the farmer, who owned the land, had grazing in the field.

One day, whilst we were enjoying our lunch in the caravan, I heard someone across the field screaming for help. I ran as hard as I could in the direction of the noise and to my horror found the farmer lying on the ground, with a young bullock, head down, kneeling on top of him. He was as white as a sheet, and was obviously in a bad way. This was no time for indecision. I put my left thumb and finger in the beast's nose, grabbed it by the horns with my right hand and heaved.

I am 6ft tall and pretty powerful, and my effort caught it off balance, then I rolled it over onto its side. The farmer scrambled to his feet and managed to find the stick with which he had been trying to defend himself. Once I saw that he wasn't seriously hurt I released the beast, which regained its feet and galloped away, aided by a hefty kick up its backside.

The farmer was very shaken and couldn't thank me enough. Apparently he had just been wandering through the field to inspect his cattle, when this particular animal had attacked him. There were a lot of flies around at the time and this can sometimes make cattle go berserk.

It was certainly lucky for him, that being a farmer myself I knew what to do – and not only that, apart from Sheila, I was the only other person within half a mile.

We were thoroughly enjoying our sailing at Bala and soon had sufficient confidence to take part in the racing. By this time I had taken part with Barry in the GP14 Northern Championships at Chasewater, and the National Championships at Holyhead so knew what it was like to twist and turn in a fleet of 100 boats.

There were many different classes of boats at Bala, so a few of the races had to be run on handicap. This meant that according to how fast your boat was, at the end of the race you either had minutes added or subtracted to your finishing time.

The largest class racing was the Albacore, which was faster than the GP14 and reputably a very good sea boat. And it could be raced with three in the crew.

We sold *Tamba* the GP14 and had a 15ft Albacore called *Miranda* built.

CHAPTER 27

A CHANGE OF HEART

It was now over 10 years since we had bought Massey House Farm. Things had changed a good deal in that time. I was still doing my daily run to Ellesmere Port, but in the beginning it used to take me 40 minutes, whereas now there were streams of holiday coaches and a general build-up of traffic, and it was taking me an hour and a half. This meant that I wasn't getting home for my dinner until about 7.30pm, and on Friday, my late night, it was 10.30pm. Not very funny after a hard day's work, particularly if the weather was bad and it was freezing or foggy.

It was all work, the only play being during the spring and autumn when we could go sailing on alternate weekends. Our social life was in ruins, or rather non-existent. All our farming neighbours normally finished work by about 6pm and could then visit their friends or generally socialise. By the time that I had reached home and had my meal, it was around 9pm – too late to go out visiting, and in any case I felt more like going to bed. Sheila and I both felt that we had reached a crossroads in life. I was at this time in my mid-forties, round about the halfway mark. I had enjoyed the challenge of the farming life, but now I had more or less realised my ambitions and transformed the farm into something to be proud of. I suppose it was a feeling of "mission accomplished and what do I do now?" There was no doubt about it, the time for decision was rapidly approaching.

I could not continue doing the two jobs with the long journeys and ever-increasing traffic. I should either have to sell my optical practice and farm full-time, or sell the farm, go back to full-time optics and move back to the Wirral. We spent endless hours working out our options. We even considered selling the milking herd and going over entirely to beef rearing. This would have eased things considerably, as I would not have been called upon to calve cows in the middle of the night, nor have the trouble of recording milk yields and other details. It would have been a risky business, as this is a long-term process with no regular money coming in, and there was no means of telling what the prices would be by the time that the cattle were ready for market. On the other hand our labour costs would have been considerably less.

Alternatively, if I sold my practice and worked full-time on the farm, I would be able to pay off my overdraft and other loans, but it would mean a considerable drop in our standard of living. By this time our two eldest children were away as boarders at expensive schools and would eventually be going on to university. There was no way would I be able to continue to meet such expenses on the income that the farm would be likely to generate. I would no longer be able to run my Jaguar(!), Sheila's help in the house would have to go and I would also have to sack two of the men. Did I want to go back to living on a shoestring and inflict these hardships on my family?

I really was in a quandary as to what to do. I loved the open-air life and the super herd that I had bred over the last ten years, but I could see that if I stayed on the farm without the considerable income which I had been injecting from optics, then I could very well be shovelling muck at the age of seventy. These thoughts were particularly engendered by the fact that nine months previously there had been an outbreak of foot and mouth disease in the district.

We had taken very stringent precautions, and of course were a closed herd, so we came through unscathed but it was heartbreaking to see the havoc it had wreaked on some of our neighbours, who had nothing now but empty fields and empty pockets.

And what about the other option, that we sell the farm, and move back to the Wirral ?

It was decided that if we were to go back to the Wirral, then we would probably go to the West Kirby area.

I had been born in Liverpool, and often as a boy, would spend many happy hours at the Pier Head watching the great Transatlantic liners being hitched up to tiny tugs and hauled out to the 'Bar' from where they would commence their long voyage to America. One of my delights was to board *The Royal Daffodil*, one of the little Mersey ferryboats and be transported across to the Wirral peninsula to Seacombe or Eastham, where we used to picnic in the woods, which in the spring were full of daffodils.

The favourite place was New Brighton, where there were boating pools, the Tower Ballroom and a zoological garden. On disembarking from the ferry you were enthralled by the sight of 'Peggy' the one-legged diver, who used to dive from the top of the landing stage to between the piers to retrieve the coins which the passengers used to throw into the water.

We thought it would be a good idea to scout out the Wirral area to get some idea of prices and types of houses which were available. I could have popped over myself to have a look around but to get there and back in my dinner hour was not very practical, so it was arranged that Sheila and her mother would drive over and see the estate agents, and get as much information as possible.

They went over on a Tuesday morning and spent the day looking around. When I got home at night, they were full of enthusiasm. One particular house they had seen was apparently quite superb.

It was situated in Caldy, which is the posh area of West Kirby. It was only four years old and was called 'Caldy Wood'. It was situated on top of the hill and had natural sandstone rockeries all around it. There was roughly an acre of land with it, mostly covered in silver birch trees, and it looked down into the woods of Caldy Manor Estate.

The house itself had four bedrooms, a super lounge with an enormous picture window, a dining room, a study and all sorts of desirable features including two bathrooms, a superb kitchen with a blue Aga cooker, a cocktail bar and a twin garage.

The crowning feature as far as Sheila was concerned was that it had double glazing and full central heating. Having endured 10 years with ice inside our bedroom window in the winter, this really did seem like heaven.

Not only did they come back with all these alluring tales about this wonder house, they had also found out that the West Kirby Sailing Club ran races out on the tide every weekend for an attractive 20-footer called a Liverpool Bay Falcon.

"Just think, instead of having to take a turn at milking the cows on a Saturday afternoon, you could be enjoying a sail – and you would be home at 6.30 in the evening, which would give you plenty of time to have a game of golf."

My farming world, by contrast, was rapidly beginning to crumble.

After a sleepless night, the next day, I decided to cancel my last appointment at Ellesmere Port and pop over to Caldy and see this house for myself. It was everything that Sheila and her mother had raved about, and I could see that we could be very happy there.

The following day I rang Manleys, the auctioneers in Whitchurch, to get some idea of what price the farm would be likely to make at auction. I did some rapid calculations and it seemed that by the time we sold the farm, all our stock and implements, and paid off all our loans, we should be left with enough money to buy Caldy Wood, or a similar property, and have a few thousand left in reserve.

It was a big decision to make. I was getting older and the thought of a luxury home, and freedom from that long frustrating journey every day, won the battle. I rang the West Kirby estate agents, and put in a bid for Caldy Wood. Drawing on past experience, I told them the offer was only open for two days. On the afternoon of the second day, the auctioneers rang my secretary to say that the offer had been accepted. I phoned Sheila straight away to tell her the good news.

When I got home that evening Sheila was wild with excitement. I was only just beginning to realise that for some time she had been yearning for the day when I would be home at a reasonable time, and not worn out and ready for bed.

The next step, of course, was to sell the farm. I put the pressure on Manleys and within a week they had auction notices in all the local newspapers.

It would mean that we would have to have three auctions: the first one to sell the farm, the second one to auction all the animals, and the third one to auction the implements and surplus household effects.

When I told the staff that we were leaving, they were absolutely crestfallen. I told them that they would all have good references and would probably be taken on by the new owners. They were inconsolable. I think they realised that it would probably be a 'proper farmer' who would be their new master, and 'proper farmers' aren't noted for their generosity.

Selling any property is a time-consuming and frustrating business – selling a farm is even worse. Showing people around, even if you only show them round the buildings and let them walk the fields on their own, can take can take ages and ages. Then of course they want to see over the house and usually make all sorts of criticisms which make you squirm.

The property auction was to take place at the Victoria Hotel in Whitchurch, in three weeks' time, after all the newspaper announcements and other publicity had hopefully done their job.

It wasn't long before the first prospective purchasers arrived. We went through all the viewing processes and left them to go over the fields themselves. They arrived back full of enthusiasm. It was a super farm, and just what they would like, but they would have to sell their smallholding first, in order to raise the capital required.

"Fat chance!" we thought, with only three weeks to go before the auction.

We had about 20 viewers before the auction. Some of them had obviously only come for a day out, and others out of sheer curiosity. It was terribly difficult to tell who was genuinely interested in purchase. We had one young couple who were really keen and liked everything about the place. We really liked their style and would have been very pleased if they had become the new owners. We had another couple who were getting married in three weeks. The bride's father, who owned a chain of furniture stores, was looking for a farm to give his daughter as a wedding present.

The bride-to-be, as she walked around the house, criticised something in every room she went in. She fairly got on Sheila's nerves and I must admit that the idea of them just walking in on the strength of 'Daddy's Money', after all our hard work, didn't make me happy.

Another interesting couple were the 'Browns of Biddulph'. They were a pleasant middle-aged couple, who owned a farm which was apparently being requisitioned for road improvements. They spent the whole of one day walking every inch of our farm when I happened to be at home. They arrived back at the house, exhausted, at about 4.30pm. They were delighted with everything and wanted all sorts of details and statistics. Sheila asked them in for tea and they settled themselves down in easy chairs, chatting away until 7pm – having by that time also consumed a couple of my malt whiskies.

Three days afterwards, when I was over in Ellesmere Port, they had been back again for further viewing. When I arrived home at 7pm, there they were, sitting in front of the fire, my bottle of malt on the table in front of them.

By this time, we were convinced that they would probably be the new owners. The day of the auction finally arrived. We had an early lunch and were just preparing to leave, when I looked out of the kitchen window.

"Do you see what I see?'"

"Why! What!'"

"The 'Browns of Biddulph' are in the yard."

We opened the door and went outside. Sure enough, there they were, poking around from one building to another. The auction was due to commence at 2.30pm and as it was now 1.45pm we climbed into our Jag and drove away to Whitchurch.

I had a few words with the auctioneer and we then went out to take our place. Sure enough, the 'Browns of Biddulph' were there, seated in the middle of the front row.

Bidding was slow to start with, but it soon heated up. By the time of the sixth bid the Browns had not made a move. It came to the eighth, and the auctioneer was raising his hammer...

"GOING! GOING! GONE!"

No! The Browns didn't put in a single bid.

And who was the winner? Why, the furniture millionaire – of course.

We heaved a sigh of relief. The price it made was not nearly as high as we had hoped for, considering the vast amount of money we had poured into the farm over the years, but we were well within our budget, and it was too late to worry about what might have been. It was a bad time to sell, just after a foot and mouth scare and the beginning of the Common Market. I felt cheated in a way – over 10 years I had worked myself into the ground, spent all the money I had earned in my optical practice, which the farm had just devoured, and in the final outcome it returned a mere pittance of £24,500. It took another 10 years before farming really took off and then farms of our size started to make a small fortune.

Having sold the farm, the next auction was for disposal of the livestock. I had told all our staff that I would keep them on and pay their full wages until the day when we had our final sale, so we had plenty of labour available for preparing the cattle for the sale ring. They had always been groomed and were washed daily, but now they really had that special attention to bring them up to show standard. Udders were clipped, tails washed in buckets of Lux and hooves were pared and polished. They really did look a picture and I was proud of them.

The day of the auction arrived and Manley's men erected a primitive sale ring just outside the shippon.

The auctioneer had a rostrum at one corner of the ring and took charge of the proceedings from there. George, our herdsman, led in the cows one at a time and the auctioneer read out all the particulars which I had prepared for him, detailing pedigree, milk yields, butterfats, etc.

One by one, my lovely herd was knocked down to the highest bidder. Most of them I could remember as tiny calves, quite a few of which I had delivered in the wee small hours of the morning. My eyes became misty, I turned away: I couldn't bear to remain there any longer. It didn't take long – within a couple of hours they had all been loaded up into cattle lorries and trailers, and were on their way to new homes. They all made good prices, but I felt desolate to see them go.

Our herd of pedigree Large White pigs was also sold at the auction. The two boars were put up separately, with the auctioneer reading out their individual pedigrees. The rest were sold in various lots such as stores, in-pig gilts etc.

We were lucky with the poultry, as they had just finished their laying term, so they were sold off as one lot to a poultry dealer.

A farm without animals is a dismal and lonely place. We had another week to go before our final auction and we had all sorts of mixed feelings:

Nostalgia for our lost dream! We had sampled a different life. A hard life, in many ways full of enigmas.

- The joy of working out in the fields of a spring morning.
- The pain of cutting and loading kale in a hard frost.
- The thrill of delivering a live heifer calf from one of your best cows.
- The despair at finding one of your gilts had lain on and killed all her litter.

All these thoughts came tumbling back.

After all, we could just have stayed at Brook House, our beautiful country estate, and enjoyed all of the 'Good Life' without any of the pitfalls.

There was still the final hurdle to leap. The farm was now empty of livestock, so all the men had to do was to prepare the machinery and implements for the final auction. A coat of paint works wonders, so I set them to work repainting the pick-up bailer in its original colours. All the other carts, tractors, etc, were treated in a similar manner. The pig arks, poultry houses and hay boxes were all scrubbed clean and creosoted.

It is amazing when you root around what you find in the way of bits and pieces which you had forgotten existed, such as racks of various medicines and drenches, clippers and veterinary instruments.

We had also decided, or rather Sheila had decided, that as part of the auction we should dispose of quite a lot of our furniture. The farmhouse had six bedrooms, two kitchens, two bathrooms, a lounge and dining room combined, and another morning room, so my dear wife told me that in our new comfortable modern house we would have no room for four-poster beds, two lounge suites and two grandfather clocks. We would have to furnish the new place with modern furniture and get rid of a lot of old rubbish.

When it came to the day of the last auction, we were blessed with a blue sky and warm sunshine, so it was decided to have all our surplus domestic gear dragged outside. There were, amongst other things, various bits of old carpet and curtain material which Sheila wanted to throw away.

"Don't throw that out, I bet they will fight over it," I insisted.

There was a large crowd in attendance, not just farmers but all their wives and families who had obviously come to look for bargains. Everyone seemed to be having a field day and thoroughly enjoying themselves. When it came to auctioning off the furniture and small items, we had to wake up some of the wives, who were sitting on the settees and easy chairs and had nodded off in the warm sunshine.

I have just unearthed a copy of the sale details (see Appendix), and I cannot believe my eyes when I see that we sold a grandfather clock, in perfect working order, for five shillings. Today it would make £1,000. The piece of old matting that Sheila wanted to throw out, made £2. The four-poster bed did not receive a single bid. We sent it to auction rooms in Chester, where I think that it made £3.

Altogether there were 100 items in the auction (see Appendix ii) and – guess what – the total amount came to £339 5s 6d! Included in the auction were:

- Two three-piece lounge suites
- One Chinese carpet
- One oak court cupboard
- One oak roll-top desk
- One oak chest
- One dining room suite
- One three-piece walnut bedroom suite
- One 12 bore shotgun

The last item I sold for £4 10s 0d to a farmer who told me that he had a gun licence. Six months later, when we had moved to Caldy, a policeman knocked on the door and told me that the farmer had not got a licence, so we were both hauled up in front of the magistrate and fined £60 each. The gun was confiscated. I was furious, as of course I had only received £4 10s 0d for it.

All the farm staff were present at the last sale, so when it was over, we asked them and the auctioneers into our big kitchen and poured them out large measures of Scotch. It was a case of goodbye and good luck. None of them knew if they were to be re-engaged by the new owners, so they would just have to wait and see. When they had all gone, we sat back feeling empty and utterly exhausted.

The next day a large furniture van arrived. The remaining furniture and all our personal possessions were loaded on the lorry and away they went to the Wirral.

There was now nothing to keep us at Massey House Farm. We had one last nostalgic look around the echoing and empty buildings, closed the doors, put our suitcases in the back of the car and drove slowly out of the farmyard on our way to a new and more luxurious life.

Jack celebrates his 85th birthday in June 2000

POSTSCRIPT

After we left the farm we had plenty of time to reminisce. In retrospect, would we have done it again? Yes, we would! Financially it had been a bit of a disaster. If I had spent all my time and energy in optics for the previous ten years, and conserved all the money which I had poured into the farm, I would have undoubtedly ended up a richer man – but money does not always bring happiness. For one thing we had been lucky in steering clear of any major disaster, such as foot and mouth disease, contagious abortion and so on, and above all we had made a lot of real friends along the way.

I was nearly forty-six when we left the farm, so was roughly halfway through my life span. As I write this book, I am now eighty-eight and Sheila is eighty-six. We have had many ensuing adventures in our latter years, but are now retired and living in what was once a fisherman's cottage on the shore of the Menai Straits in Anglesey.

Llanfaes
Beaumaris
March 2004

APPENDICES

(i) Transcript of sale catalogue, 1951
(ii) Transcript of auction proceeds, 1961
(iii) Plan of Massey House Farm buildings

IT'S MUCK YOU WANT!

NORTH SHROPSHIRE
In an Agricultural District of Repute

A VALUABLE FREEHOLD

Dairy or Mixed Farm

Extending to

123 Acres

MASSEY HOUSE FARM

OTHERWISE KNOWN AS

"UPPER TILSTOCK PARK FARM"

NEAR WHITCHURCH

WITH VACANT POSSESSION   FREE OF TENANTRIGHT

TO BE SOLD BY AUCTION AT

THE VICTORIA HOTEL - WHITCHURCH

— ON —

FRIDAY, 9TH MARCH, 1951

SOLICITOR	AUCTIONEER
W. GOUGH THOMAS ESQ	HENRY MANLEY & SONS LTD
WILLOW STREET,	WHITCHURCH, CREWE, NANTWICH
	AND MARKET DRAYTON

WHITCHURCH HERALD LIMITED

(i) This page and following three pages, transcript of sale catalogue

By instructions of Mr. W. Thomas, the owner-occupier:

TILSTOCK PARK

NEAR WHITCHURCH, SHROPSHIRE

Distant 3 miles from the Town of Whitchurch
7 miles from Wem and 9 miles from Ellesmere,
Situate at Hollinwood with long frontages to the Tilstock Road

---

A Freehold

DAIRY OR MIXED FARM

of excellent repute, known as

MASSEY HOUSE FARM

otherwise
"UPPER TILSTOCK PARK FARM"
Extending to an area of

122 Acres 3 Roods 23 perches

(or thereabouts)

WITH VACANT POSSESSION
Free of Valuable Tenantright

To be offered For Sale by Auction by

HENRY MANLEY & SONS, Ltd

At the VICTORIA HOTEL, WHITCHURCH
On Friday, 9th March, 1951, at 3.30pm

(Subject to conditions)

Permits to view and any further information may be obtained from the Auctioneers' Offices, Whitchurch (Tel. 19 and 357), Crewe (Tel. 2654 and 2651) and Market Drayton (Tel. 2206) or the Vendor's Solicitor:
W. GOUGH THOMAS, Esq
Bulkeley Chambers
Willow Street
ELLESMERE (Tel. 13), Shropshire

IT'S MUCK YOU WANT!

NORTH SHROPSHIRE

PARTICULARS OF

MASSEY HOUSE FARM

otherwise known as
"UPPER TILSTOCK PARK FARM"
3 miles from Whitchurch
Extending to

122 Acres   3 Rods   23 Perches
(or thereabouts)

WITH VACANT POSSESSION
Free of Tenantright

The Farm is pleasantly situated at Hollinwood. The House and Buildings which are set back from the road are approached by a short Drive.

THE FARM RESIDENCE, which faces south and is fronted by a Lawn and small Garden is of attractive structure in brick with slated roof.

The Accommodation comprises:

Tiled Entrance Hall with cloak rail.

SITTING ROOM 16ft. x 14ft. 3in. having a modern cream tiled firegrate with raised hearth.

DINING ROOM 18ft. x 14ft. with a similar firegrate.

The Front Staircase leads to a compact main Landing from which a central passage traverses the First Floor to the rear Landing and Staircase.

FIVE GOOD SIZED BEDROOMS all with fitted grates.   BOXROOM.

The Domestic Offices comprise a COMFORTABLE LIVING ROOM with oak beamed ceiling and "Swinton" patent Cooking Range and hot water boiler. China pantry. Pantry with Shelving. Store Room. Dairy with Firegrate. Press House. Store Room with two-tier shelving. Wash House with Two bricked Wash Boilers, Sink and Draining Board. Cellar. Lean-to Refrigerator Shed.

The Water Supply for drinking purposes is from a pump well in the Houseyard. A Rotary Pump in the Wash House supplies water for domestic purposes.

IT'S MUCK YOU WANT!

THE FARM BUILDINGS which are conveniently placed and mainly brick built with tiled roofs comprise:

SHIPPONS FOR 43 CATTLE, Two Young Stock Sheds, 2 Loose Boxes, Calf Kit, Large Barn, Two Granaries, Two Root Houses, Stabling for 4 Horses, Garage, Range of Three Piggeries, Duck Cote.

STACKYARD containing 7-Bay Dutch Barn on steel pillars, each bay 6yds. x 5yds.

THE LAND is a deep medium loam of natural fertility, mainly under grass, with a plentiful water supply. It is especially convenient for management and well adapted to modern mechanised farming. The fields are level, conveniently sized and have long road frontages.

SCHEDULE

O.S. No.	Description	Area
1678	Hill Field	19.181
1679	Park Field	21.738
1681	Long Field	18.178
1681 a	Pond	.150
1789 (pt)	Night Pasture	15.332
1790	Field	3.195
1791	House, Buildings and Stackyard	2.034
1793	Field	6.508
1794	Field	5.420
1807	Field	5.475
1808	Garden Croft	1.377
1658 (pt)	Part Big Stockings	3.305
1664	Part Broad Leasows	3.837
1675	Little Stockings	7.380
1676	Chapel Field	9.678
1676 a	Pond	.116
	TOTAL ACRES	122.904

122 ACRES   3 ROODS   23 PERCHES

IT'S MUCK YOU WANT!

SALE OF HOUSEHOLD FURNITURE
AND CERTAIN FARM IMPLEMENTS
AT MASSEY HOUSE FARM
FOR MR. J. E. ORRELL
ON SATURDAY, 15th APRIL, 1961.

LOT NO.	DESCRIPTION	£:	s:	d.
111.	Pig Weighing Machine	5:	-:	-.
112.	McConnell Mounted Saw Bench	29:	-:	-.
113.	Ferguson Pulley	11:	-:	-.
114.	Ferguson Power Takeoff Unit	3:	10:	-.
115.	Ferguson Earth Scoop	9:	-:	-.
116.	Ferguson Transport Box	8:	10:	-.
119.	Set of Ferguson Triple Spiked Harrows	11:	-:	-.
120.	Set of Ferguson Spring Tyne Cultivator	32:	-:	-.
121.	Set of Ferguson Disc Harrows	50:	-:	-.
123.	Ferguson 3-row Ridger	22:	-:	-.
131.	Parker "Mini-Giant" Concrete Mixer, model 2T	60:	-:	-.
136.	Single Cow Trailer	31:	-:	-.
138.	Ferguson, hydraulic tipping 2-wheel Tractor Trailer	91:	-:	-.
196/205.	9 Vic Hallam Night Arks @ £9. 5s.	83:	-:	-.
	1 - ditto - @ £9. 7s. 6d.	9:	7:	6.
227.	Sectional Wooden and Asbestos-roofed Poultry House, 15ft x 12ft with nest boxes, etc	46:	-:	-.
		£501:	12:	6.
FURNITURE				
402.	Tricycle	2:	15:	-.
403.	Chest and Trouser Press		1:	-.
404.	Poufee		2:	-.
	c/f	2:	18:	-.

(ii) This page and following pages, transcript of auction proceeds

IT'S MUCK YOU WANT!

LOT NO.	DESCRIPTION	£	S:	d.
	b/f	2:	18:	-.
405.	Carpet Sweeper		1:	-.
406.	Plant Pots		6:	-.
407.	Fire Guard		1:	-.
408.	Mirror		7:	6.
409.	High Chair, 3 Kerbs		7:	6.
411.	Set of Steps		12:	6.
413.	Boys Bicycle	1:	10:	-.
414.	Girls Bicycle		15:	-.
415.	3-piece Walnut Bedroom Suite	17:	-:	-.
415a.	Bedstead	3:	-:	-.
416.	2-piece Bedroom Suite	6:	-:	-.
417.	Small Antique Swing Mirror	6:	-:	-.
418.	Oak Chest-of-Drawers	10:	-:	-.
419.	Grandfather Clock		5:	-.
421.	Oak Bureau Bookcase	7:	10:	-.
422.	Barometer & 2 Pictures	1:	10:	-.
423.	Food Mixer	12:	-:	-.
424.	Percolator, etc		14:	-.
425.	Books		1:	-.
426.	Oak Sideboard	8:	-:	-.
427.	Table Lamp		12:	-.
428.	Mantel Clock		10:	-.
429.	Snap Top Table	2:	12:	-.
430.	Galleon, Bagatelle Board, etc.		2:	6.
431.	Lloyd Loom Chair	1:	-:	-.
432.	Tilley lamp		5:	-.
433.	- ditto - and Other		5:	-.
434.	Kitchen Cabinet	5:	-:	-.
435.	Calor Gass Cooker		10:	-.
436.	Bread Slicer		5:	-.
437.	Cot and Mattress		2:	6.
438.	Radiogram	9:	5:	-.
439.	Oak Court Cupboard	18:	-:	-.
440.	Oak Roll Top Desk	30:	-:	-.
441.	Lloyd Loom Linen Basket	3:	5:	-.
442.	Lloyd Loom Table	3:	-:	-.
	c/f £153:		12:	6.

IT'S MUCK YOU WANT!

LOT NO.	DESCRIPTION	£:	s:	d.
443.	Oak Chair		7:	6.
444.	Dressing Stool	2:	-:	-.
445.	Oak Coffee Table	3:	5:	-.
446.	Brass Chestnut Roaster	1:	5:	-.
447.	Oak Occasional Table	2:	10:	-.
447a.	Electric Iron		1:	-.
448.	Roller Skates		7:	6.
449.	Gramaphone		10:	-.
450.	Oak Drop Leaf table	3:	-:	-.
451.	Chest of 2 drawers		12:	6.
452.	Cupboard		10:	-.
453.	Toilet Ware		1:	-.
454.	Fire Guard		1:	-.
455.	Oak Chest	4:	-:	-.
457.	3 Dining Chairs	1:	10:	-.
458.	4 Dining Chairs @ £2. 2. 6.	8:	10:	-.
459.	Bathroom Stool	1:	-:	-.
460.	12 Bore Shot Gun	4:	10:	-.
461.	Gun		7:	6.
462.	Sword)	1:	2:	6.
463.	Ornamental Spears)			
464.	Oak Table	1:	-:	-.
465.	Card table		4:	6.
467.	Electric Fire		5:	-.
468.	- ditto -	2:	-:	-.
469.	Haversacks, etc		1:	-.
470.	3-piece lounge suite	10:	-:	-.
471.	Single Bedstead		10:	-.
472.	- ditto -	1:	10:	-.
473.	Double Bedstead		10:	-.
474.	Feather Bed		15:	-.
474a.	Mattress	3:	10:	-.
476.	2 pieces of Coconut Matting	2:	-:	-.
477.	2 pieces - ditto -		10:	-.
478.	1 piece - ditto -	3:	10:	-.
479.	1 piece - ditto -	3:	10:	-.
480.	Landing Runner	1:	-:	-.
481.	Chinese carpet	4:	-:	-.

c/f £213: 18: 6.

IT'S MUCK YOU WANT!

LOT NO.	DESCRIPTION	£:	s:	d.
482.	Wool Rug		12:	6.
483.	2 Mats	1:	-:	-.
484.	Wool Carpet	3:	-:	-.
485.	Chinese Carpet	43:	-:	-.
486.	Wool Carpet	4:	-:	-.
487.	Oak Draw-Leaf Table	3:	-:	-.
488.	Electric Cooker	45:	-:	-.
491.	Pair of Red Curtains		10:	-.
492.	- ditto -	2:	10:	-.
493.	- ditto - and Pelmet		15:	-.
494.	- ditto -	1:	2:	6.
495.	- ditto -		15:	-.
496.	Pair of Curtains and pelmet	1:	12:	6.
497.	- ditto -		5:	-.
498.	- ditto -	2:	5:	-.
499.	- ditto -	1:	15:	-.
500.	- ditto -	1.	2:	6.
501.	2 Pillows and 1 Curtain		5.	-.
502.	2 Tables		10:	-.
		£339:	5:	6.

SUMMARY

Implements	501:	12:	6.
Furniture	339:	5:	6.
	840:	18:	-.
To Our Special Commission at 2½%	21:	-:	-.
	819:	18:	-.

HENRY MANLEY & SONS LTD
AUCTIONEERS AND VALUERS
WHITCHURCH, CREWE, NANTWICH
AND MARKET DRAYTON

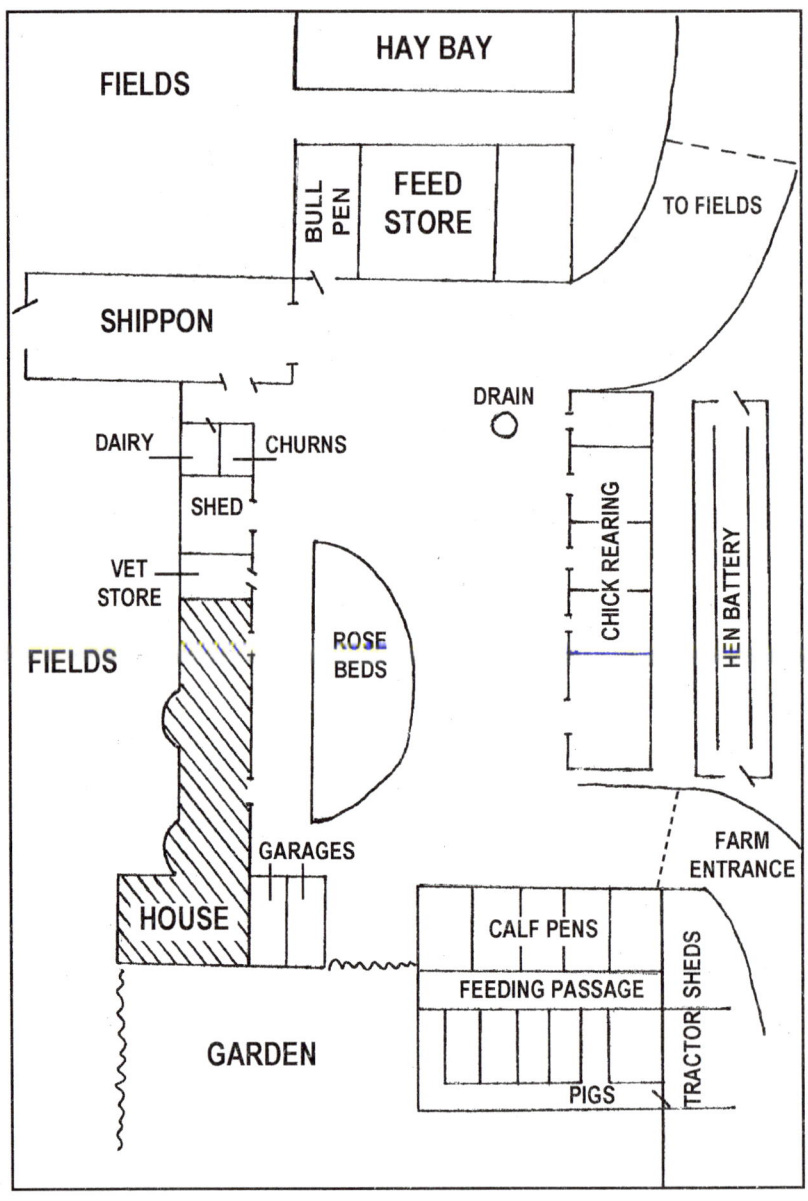

(iii) Plan of Massey House Farm buildings